DOES THE UNIVERSE HAVE A SOUL?

Rabbi Michael Gold, PhD

Illustrations by Carly Shooster

Paper back ISBN-13: 978-1-946469-74-8
Hardcover ISBN-13: 978-1-946469-22-9

ShelteringTree.Earth, LLC Publishing
PO Box 973, Eagle Lake, FL 33839

Did you enjoy this book?
We love to hear from our readers.
Please visit the author at
ShelteringTreeMedia.com

About the Cover:
Artist Sergey Nivens
Title of Piece Magnetic Soul Cosmos
Location Australia

DEDICATION

To my Children and Grandchildren, present and future.

Your Souls are Gifts from God.

CONTENTS

Introduction

Does the universe have a soul? This is the question we will explore in this book.

We will explore this question through the eyes of religion. I have been a rabbi serving congregations for over forty years, so I will certainly focus on my own religious tradition, Judaism. But I am also a professor of religion and will seek insights not only from the Western Abrahamic religious traditions of Judaism, Christianity, and Islam, but such Eastern traditions as Hinduism, Buddhism and Daoism.

We will explore this question through the eyes of philosophy. I wrote my PhD dissertation on process philosophy and Jewish mysticism and have been a professor of philosophy over ten years. I understand philosophy can never give us a final answer, but it can sharpen our thinking by asking stimulating questions. The Socratic method, at the heart of philosophy, is building dialogues through challenging questions.

We will explore this question through the eyes of science. I have learned much from the great Jewish philosopher Maimonides (1138-1204), where he compared the Biblical view of creation to Aristotle's view of an eternal universe. He took the Biblical view on faith, but then taught, if Aristotle should be proven correct, we would need to reinterpret the Bible to agree with Aristotle.[1] I see no conflict between religion and science. Religion should always be interpreted with the best of science.

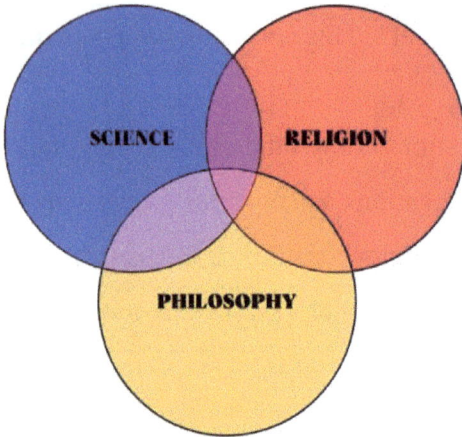

As this Venn diagram illustrates, I see myself as standing in the middle, where religion, philosophy, and science meet. (Diagram drawn by my son-in-law Darren Simons.)

*   *   *   *   *   *   *

Does the universe have a soul?

Before we can answer this, we must define the word *soul*. We will do this in chapter 1. But before we can define soul, we must explore the issue of mind. And that is a daunting task. What does it mean to have a mind?

Mind. Consciousness. Sentience. Awareness. Subjectivity. What do they mean? Each of us is aware that we are conscious. We have a mind. We have a self that is aware of the world around us. Even when we sleep, we seem to be conscious. We dream and after we awake, we often are aware of those dreams.

We have a will and seem to be able to make choices about our lives. Volition appears to be central to the idea of mind. Of course, many philosophers and scientists argue that free will is an illusion. Our choices are the result of our genetic code and our upbringing; nature and nurture, with no free will. But at least according to our subjective insight, we seem to make choices. And we must live with the consequences of those choices.

At the dawn of modern philosophy, the French thinker René Descartes (1596-1650) was searching for a foundation for all knowledge. Is there anything we can know beyond all doubt? He began with radical doubt, doubting everything he ever knew, everything he had ever learned. He doubted everything he had learned through his religious upbringing. He doubted mathematical truths he had learned. He even doubted that he had a body. Maybe an evil demon was tricking him. (Demons will become a central part of this book.) Maybe we are simply a Brain in a Vat, to quote a classical thought experiment. The *Matrix*[2] movie series, where our minds are really computer programs and our bodies computer simulations, is based on Descartes' philosophy.

Descartes asked if there were anything that is beyond doubt, something he knew with absolute certainty. Then he came up with one of the most famous lines in the history of philosophy, *cogito ergo sum*, "I think, therefore I am."[3] There was no doubt that he was doubting; he was thinking. The fact that we have a mind - consciousness and awareness - seems beyond doubt. For Descartes, it was the foundation of all knowledge. Later Descartes would prove we have a body, but this body was a totally separate substance from the mind. He was the first modern dualist, believer that mind and body are two separate substances. We will say more about this later.

Each of us has a mind; we are thinking beings. But this raises more questions than it answers. Where did this mind come from? Did it exist before we were born? If so, where did it exist? Is there some spiritual realm of minds without bodies? Will the mind still be here after we die? If so, where will it go? Will it return to that spiritual realm? Is this the essence of a soul, something that exists beyond our physical body, present before we were born and after we die.

Or is our mind just a function of our body, the way our brain works? Did our mind only appear when our brain appeared, somewhere about six weeks after conception? And will our mind die when our brain dies? What if we are brain dead, but our body is being kept alive by a machine? Does our mind still exist? Or does brain death imply mind death?

I know I have a mind. But what about other people? Do they also have minds? Solipsism is the belief that only I have a mind, no one else does. But how can I ever know if other people have minds? I can see other people's bodies, but not their inner subjective experiences. Maybe other people are just robots or androids.

Philosophers speak of *Philosophical Zombies*. These are not the brain eating monsters of the movies. Rather, philosophical zombies look just like people, act just like people but have no mind, no inner awareness. If a Philosophical Zombie touches a hot stove, it will pull its hand away and say "ouch." But there is no inner feeling of pain, no inner feeling of any kind. A Philosophical Zombie behaves like a human being but lacks the essence of a human being, a mind. It has no inner subjective experiences. Could such Philosophical Zombies exist? The philosopher of mind David Chalmers (b. 1966) used this idea to prove that the mind must be more than body.[4]

We humans may be conscious, but what about animals? Descartes believed that animals have no consciousness, they were automatons or little robots. To Descartes, since animals have no soul, they have no mind. Even in his own day, most people believed Descartes was wrong. It seems obvious to us that our dogs and cats are conscious beings. The founder of the ethical theory utilitarianism, Jeremy Bentham (1748–1832), famously said that animals may not be able to reason, but they can suffer.[5] Therefore, ethics must be concerned not only with the treatment of humans but with animals. Bentham invented an entire ethical system, utilitarianism, which is concerned with the treatment of all sentient beings, humans and animals.

But what do we mean by sentient beings? If animals are conscious beings, how far down the ladder of animal life does consciousness exist? Do primates have minds? Dogs and cats? Reptiles? Birds? Fish? Insects? Bacteria? Viruses? If life evolved through natural selection as Charles Darwin (1809–1882) taught, at what level of life did mind enter the animal kingdom? Does mind require a certain level of neural complexity? Or is mind present all the way down?

If animals have minds, what about machines? Could a robot have a soul? Could we build a computer with subjective awareness? This is a favorite theme of science fiction writers. From Arthur C. Clarke's *2001: A Space Odyssey*[6] and Stanley Kubrick's film adaption[7], to Isaac Asimov's *I, Robot*[8], from Steven Spielberg *A.I. Artificial Intelligence*[9] to the hit television show, *Westworld*[10], from Philip K. Dick's novel *Do Androids Dream of Electric Sheep?*[11] to the *Blade Runner*[12] movie adaptations of the novel, we are fascinated with the question whether machines have consciousness. Certainly, we can build computers that imitate many features of the human mind. Computers do pattern recognition; our smart phone has software to recognize our faces. Computers can do calculations far more quickly and accurately than we can. Computers can observe the world and take in input. They can do cognition, processing information to make decisions. Think about the way our GPS (Global Positioning System) can calculate the shortest route to drive to our destination.

Nonetheless, does our computer have self-awareness or consciousness? Could a computer say as Descartes did, "I think therefore I am?" Is there an "I" there, a subjective sense of self? When our computer does work, is it aware of what it is doing? Chalmers, who we discussed regarding Philosophical Zombies, speaks of the soft problem of consciousness and the hard problem of consciousness.[13] The soft problem of consciousness is the study of those parts of the mind which a computer can imitate – pattern recognition, calculations, perception, memory, cognition. The hard problem of consciousness is the study of subjective awareness, what philosophers call *qualia*. How can we understand the ability of the mind to experience seeing a rainbow, hearing a symphony, tasting a cup of coffee, smelling popcorn at the movie theater, or feeling the fur of a kitten? According to Chalmers, these are the questions of philosophy of mind that are far more difficult to comprehend.

*   *   *   *   *   *   *

There is another difficult question of mind. Do I share a mind with others? The psychologist Carl Jung (1875–1961) spoke of a collective consciousness. He was amazed by the way cultures throughout the world share certain archetypes. Archetypes are images or paradigms out of which religious traditions form; for example, the hero, the mother, the trickster, the jester, and the sage. Our psyches grow out of this collective consciousness through a process he called individualization. We establish a persona or mature self from this collective psyche.

If there is a collective consciousness as Jung and others have claimed, then consciousness exists beyond our individual brains. It is non-localized. Descartes has already hinted about the non-locality of mind. Body is *res extensa* or an extended thing. Bodies take up space. In contrast, mind is *res cogitans* or a thinking thing, existing beyond any space. Is Descartes correct in saying that mind does not take up space? Unlike the brain, the mind has no location. If so, mind must be more than the brain. Why have so many people who had near death experiences spoken of their mind leaving their body? Why do they describe their mind floating above, perceiving doctors working on their bodies? What is the relationship between brain and mind?

If minds exist beyond brains, beyond any particular location in space, can two minds touch outside space? Does extrasensory perception (E.S.P.) exist, where people who are physically separated can sense each other's minds. Why does it often happen that we think about someone who lives out of town, and out of nowhere, they telephone?

Is mind non-local? If we are to speak about non-locality, we must mention quantum theory. Quantum theory, the fundamental theory about the basic particles of the universe, is built on non-locality. A single particle of light (photon) can go through two separated slits in a wall at the same time. It has no fixed location. One of the strange results of quantum theory is that two particles that are widely separated can instantaneously affect one another. Albert Einstein (1879-1955) used this strange phenomenon to try to disprove quantum mechanics. He called it "spooky action at a distance." In the end, scientists have proven Einstein wrong. In quantum theory, there is no locality. Particles that are light years apart can act as if they are touching, influencing one another.

The issue of consciousness is vital to quantum theory. Until a mind perceives it, particles of matter exist in a ghost like superposition of waves. Only when perceived by an observer does this wave equation collapse, giving us information about the particle. According to Noble Laureate physicist Eugene Wigner (1902–1937), it is consciousness that causes the wave to collapse and gives the particle a particular location or momentum. Wigner wrote, "I believe the present laws of physics are at least incomplete without a translation into terms of mental phenomena."[14]

This leads to one of the strangest thought experiments in physics. Edwin Schrödinger (1887-1961) imagined a closed box with a radioactive substance which might or might not give off a particle. If it gives off a radioactive particle, it will release poison gas within the box. Until a conscious mind looks at it, the substance exists in a superimposed position if giving off a particle or not giving off a particle, of releasing the poison or not releasing it. Both exist at the same time. Now Schrödinger imagined a poor cat in the box. If the poison is released, the cat is dead; if not it is alive. The cat exists in a superimposed position of being both alive and dead at the same time. Only when a mind looks at the box does the wave collapse, and we can find the fate of Schrödinger's Cat.

In the light of quantum theory, consciousness seems to be much more than a function of our individual brains. Matter as we know it only exists when a conscious mind observes it. Consciousness seems to be fundamental to the universe. Matter seems to only exist when a mind perceives it. But of course, this was the basis of Einstein's challenge to quantum theory. According to one story, Einstein asked physicist Abraham Pais, "Is the moon there when nobody is looking at it?"[15]

*   *   *   *   *   *   *

One of the most fascinating aspects of this study of consciousness is the number of thought experiments the discussion generates. Thought experiments, what Einstein called *Gedankenexperiment*, are powerful tools in both science and philosophy. Einstein developed special relativity by imagining travelling alongside a ray of light. He developed the concept of general relativity by imagining people inside a falling elevator.

We have already considered several such thought experiments. We have spoken about the Brain in the Vat, Philosophical Zombies, Schrödinger's Cat, and the Falling Elevator. Before we are finished, we will speak about Plato's Cave, Achilles and the Tortoise, Aristotle's Great Chain of Being, Galileo's Gravity, The Floating Man, The Ghost in the Machine, The Experience Machine, Zhuangzi's Butterfly, The Turning Test, Super Spartans, Buridan's Ass, Mary's Room, The Chinese Room, The Ship of Theseus, Leibniz's Mill, What it's Like to be a Bat, the Beetle in the Box, Uncovering Holy Sparks, and *Atman* is *Brahman*. These fascinating thought experiments will be a central theme throughout this book.

We will attempt to answer all of these questions. Our explanation will be divided into three parts, based on the three-fold division within metaphysics. (In philosophy, metaphysics is the study of reality.) We will first look at dualism, the idea that reality consists of two substances - mind and matter. This is the approach of most Western religions such as Judaism, Christianity, and Islam. It is also the approach of the Greek philosopher Plato. But this idea was challenged by his student Aristotle.

We will then look at materialism, the idea that only matter exists. This is the approach of most modern scientists and philosophers. We will study the problem that, if only matter exists, how does that matter create a mind. We will explore each of the three answers provided by philosophers – behaviorism, mind-brain identity theory, and functionalism.

Finally, we will look at idealism, the idea that only mind exists. This is the approach of many Eastern religions such as Hinduism and Buddhism, as well as many mystics. It is also the view of some Western thinkers such as the empiricist George Berkeley (1685–1753). Quantum theory, with its requirement of a conscious observer, also seems to point to this approach.

There are problems with all three approaches. But in the end, we will try to answer the question, *does the universe have a soul?*

Part 1: Dualism

Dualism teaches that the universe consists of two separate substances: the material and the spiritual, mind and matter, or body and soul. If you practice one of the Western faiths of the Abrahamic tradition – Judaism, Christianity, or Islam, you are probably a dualist. If you are follower of the great Greek philosopher Plato, you are probably also a dualist. And if you are an adherent to the father of modern Western philosophy René Descartes, you are probably a dualist.

The Western religious traditions, Plato, and Descartes agree that we are made of two separate parts. We have a body which begins to develop at conception and continues until we die. Then that body disintegrates. But we also have a soul, which these faiths believe to be immortal. It was there before we were born and will continue to exist after we die. In fact, this description gives us the definition of a soul: a spiritual substance that existed before we were born and will continue to exist after we die. Some would use the language that we are bodies that possess a soul. Others would use the language that we are souls who are embodied. In a saying often attributed to C.S. Lewis (1898-1963), "You don't have a soul. You are a soul. You have a body."[16] Either way, we humans consist of two parts. This idea has been deeply influential in Western thought.

Where did this idea of body and soul come from? Is it in the Bible? As we shall see, that is not clear. Let us begin with an exploration of the Hebrew Bible, what Christians call the Old Testament and Jews simply call *Tanach* or Hebrew Scripture.

Chapter 1
The Breath of God: The Soul in the Bible

The Roman emperor Antoninos confronted Rabbi Judah the Prince. He claimed that both the body and soul could exempt themselves from judgment for sin. The body could say, without the soul I would just lie here like a lump of clay. The soul could say, without the body I could just fly away. Each alone is innocent from any sin.

Rabbi Judah answered, it is like two watchmen of a fig field, one blind and one lame. When figs are stolen, both plead not guilty. The blind watchman says, I cannot see to steal the figs. The lame watchman says, I cannot walk to steal the figs. They are brought before a judge, who replies that they worked together. The lame watchman climbed onto the shoulders of the blind watchman, and together they stole the figs. So too, the body and the soul work together when they sin in this world. (Talmud Sanhedrin 31a-b)

I live in southern Florida. Part of the reality of being a rabbi here is how often I am asked to officiate at funerals, often for complete strangers. I meet with the family to get the story of their loved one's life. Often, they ask me the inevitable questions: do I believe that their loved one's soul still exists somewhere? Will they see their loved one again? Is there life after death?

I always answer, "Yes." I do not believe that the death of the body is the end of everything. There is a part of us that continues to exist. After all, I am a rabbi and a practicing Jew. Nonetheless, an authentic study of Jewish tradition does not give such a clear answer.

The Soul in Judaism

Each morning before beginning my daily prayers, I recite two separate blessings out of the *Siddur* (Hebrew prayerbook). The first blessing thanks God for creating my body with many channels and openings. If one of those openings is closed that should be open or open that should be closed, I could not exist in the world. The blessing ends by my giving thanks to God for the miracle of my body. I feel deeply blessed whenever my body works properly.

But according to the prayerbook, I am more than a body. The second blessing says that the soul God gave me is pure. God implanted it within me, will guard it within me, and one day God will take it from me. But not to worry, in the end, God will place it once again within my newly resurrected body. Each day I thank God for my soul. The body may exist temporarily, but the soul exists permanently.

Of course, my body and soul are intimately linked together while I am alive, so that it is hard to know where one ends and the other begins. They certainly work together. This was taught in the Talmudic story about the two watchmen mentioned at the beginning of the chapter. The body and the soul work together when they sin in this world. To be fair, I should say that the body and the soul also work together to perform good deeds in this world.

The body and soul are linked, but only for a limited amount of time. The body is a physical thing and by the laws of entropy, all physical things must eventually break down. As the poet W.B. Yeats (1865–1939) wrote in his poem *The Second Coming*, "Things fall apart, the centre cannot hold."[17] The body must die. The soul is a spiritual thing which our tradition teaches is eternal. This eternal soul must have come from somewhere and must return to somewhere. But where? Where did the idea of these two separate entities come from?

The Western spiritual traditions teach that the soul is an entity which existed before birth and will exist after death. Again, turning to my own tradition, a number of Rabbinic passages support this idea. The Talmud (*Yebamot* 62b) teaches that God keeps a storehouse called *guf* of all the souls waiting to be born. (The term *guf* has the strange double meaning in Hebrew; it can also be translated as *body*.) The final Messianic Age will only come when all of these souls are born into this world.

Another wonderful passage can be found in the *Zohar,* the great book of Jewish mysticism).

> *At the time when God desired to create the universe, it came up in His will before Him, and He formed all the souls which were destined to be allotted to the children of men. The souls were all*

before Him in the forms which they were afterwards destined to bear inside the human body. God looked at each one of them, and He saw that many of them would act corruptly in the world. When the time of each arrived, it was summoned before God, who said to it: "Go to such and such a part of the universe, enclose thyself in such and such a body." But the soul replied: "O sovereign of the universe, I am happy in my present world, and I desire not to leave it for some other place where I shall be enslaved and become soiled." Then the Holy One (blessed be He) replied: "From the day of thy creation thou hast had no other destiny than to go into the universe whither I send thee." The soul, seeing that it must obey, sorrowfully took the way to earth and came down to dwell in our midst. (Zohar II 96b)

But the time of dwelling in this world is only temporary. The Talmud teaches, "Rabbi Jacob said, this world is like a vestibule before the World-to-Come; prepare yourself in the vestibule, so that you may enter the banqueting-hall." (*Avot* 4:16) What is that World-to-Come like? The Talmud teaches "Rav taught, This world is not like the World to Come. In the World to Come there is no eating and no drinking, no sexual activity and no business, no jealousy, hatred, or rivalry. Rather the righteous sit with their crowns on their heads and delight in the divine presence." (*Berahkoht* 17a), In the World-to-Come, all physical activity will cease. It is a perfectly spiritual place, in keeping with our spiritual nature. (Personally, I find the idea somewhat boring. I would rather be in this material world.)

Our soul is a spiritual entity that existed before we were born. It comes into our body during our lifetime. Then it returns to that spiritual place after we die. But where did this strange idea come from? As we shall see, it is not clearly from the Bible.

The Biblical View

The Bible does speak about the soul. But the Biblical idea is far different from the soul as described above.

In fact, there are three terms the Bible uses for a soul. The most frequent is *nefesh,* which comes from a Hebrew root meaning "to rest." When God created the universe, the Torah teaches that God *shavat v'yinafash* "ceased work and rested" (Exodus 31:17). When God created each of the animals, it became a *nefesh chaya* "living soul." "Everything which the man called each living soul *(nefesh chaya)* became its name" (Genesis 2:19). Part of God came to rest in each living creature which animates it. The term *nefesh* refers to that which animates a living thing; thqt which gives it life. It is not a separate entity that exists independently of the animal, but a force which brings the animal to life. Perhaps the best metaphor is the hardware and software of the modern computer. If the animal's physical body is the hardware, the *nefesh* is the software. Just as computer hardware cannot run without software, so an animal's body cannot function without a *nefesh.*

The Bible uses a second term for that force which animates an animal, *ruach* or spirit. In fact, the Bible sometimes uses these two terms *nefesh* and *ruach* interchangeably. For example, the book of Job teaches, "In whose hand is the soul (*nefesh*) of every living thing, and the spirit (*ruach*) of all mankind" (Job 12:10). The Torah speaks of the spirit of God *Ruach Elohim* that existed before creation, that hovered over the waters. (Genesis 1:2). Again, life is something animated by that spirit of God. The French philosopher Henri Bergson (1859–1941) shared a similar idea when he taught that all life contains an *Élan Vital* "an animating force."

The Torah uses a third term, which is reserved for the souls of human beings, *neshama* or breath. God shaped humans out of clay and breathed into them a breath of life. "The Lord God formed the man from the dust of the earth and He breathed into his nostrils a breath of life (*neshama*) and the man became a living soul (*nefesh chaya*)" (Genesis 2:7).

Each of these words – *nefesh*, *ruach*, and *neshama* – refer to something that animates a body, gives it life. To return to our metaphor, it is like software. But computer software only functions if there is hardware to run it. Software may exist on a code somewhere on a disk. But it has no real function until it becomes part of the operating system of the hardware.

If the human soul is the breath of God, what happens to it when we die? The book of Ecclesiastes has a clear answer. "The dust returns to the earth as it was, and the spirit (*ruach*) returns to

God Who gave it" (Ecclesiastes 12:7). The human soul has no independent existence. It returns to its spiritual source. The breath of God returns to God.

The Bible uses another phrase to speak about death – to sleep with one's fathers. "So David slept with his fathers and was buried in the City of David" (I Kings 2:10). "So Solomon slept with his fathers and was buried in the City of his father David, and his son Rehoboam succeeded him as king" (I Kings 11:43). To die is to sleep. Shakespeare powerfully says this is Hamlet's famous soliloquy,

> To die, to sleep.
> To sleep, perchance to dream - ay, there's the rub.
> For in the sleep of death, what dreams may come,
> When we have shuffled off this mortal coil.[18]

According to the Bible, when we die, we peacefully sleep. No one wants to be awoken from such a sleep. Perhaps this image is best portrayed in the Bible in the story of King Saul and the Witch of Endor. Saul, frightened by the Philistines and seeking advice, uses the witch to conjure up the soul of the dead prophet Samuel. But Samuel is deeply angered at being roused from his sleep. "Why have you disturbed me by bringing me up" (I Samuel 28:15). Samuel rebukes Saul and tells him he will lose the kingship. The message of the Bible seems clear: when the dead are asleep with their fathers, they should not be disturbed.

Group Justice and Individual Justice

The Bible presents a very different image from that of classical Rabbinic Judaism. The soul is the breath of God which returns to its source. The body sleeps with its fathers, not to be disturbed. Where did the idea of an eternal soul come from? Allow me to present my own theory. It involved a change in Biblical religion. The Bible evolved from an emphasis on group justice to an emphasis on individual justice.

Originally the Bible speaks of group justice. Reward and punishment are meted out to an entire community. This is made explicit in the section of Deuteronomy which Jews recite morning and evening, the second paragraph of the *Sh'ma*. "If you obey the commandments which I enjoin you today, to love the Lord your God and serve Him with all your heart and all your soul, I will grant the rain for your field in its season, the early rain and the late rain, and you shall gather your grain and wine and oil" (Deuteronomy 11:13-14). The reward comes to the community as a whole. The passage continues with the punishment for not obeying God's commandments. Reward and punishment are for the group, not for individuals.

We see this idea throughout the five books of the Torah. The flood of Noah, the Tower of Babel, the Golden Calf, and the many stories of wandering through the wilderness show group punishment. Meanwhile, there is the ongoing promise of entering the land as a group reward. People are not judged as individuals but as part of the group. But this would radically change with the Babylonian exile.

Ezekiel, the great prophet of the early exile, introduces a new idea, individual reward and punishment. "The soul that sins, shall die. The son shall not bear the iniquity of the father, neither shall the father bear the iniquity of the son; the righteousness of the righteous shall be upon him, and the wickedness of the wicked shall be upon him" (Ezekiel 18:20). People are rewarded or punished for their own sins. There is a clear religious turn to the individual rather than the group. But this creates a serious problem. Too frequently in this world, bad things happen to good people while good things happen to bad people. If death means sleeping with our fathers, where is the justice? When does the reward and punishment occur?

The Western Abrahamic religions - Judaism, Christianity, and Islam - developed a powerful answer. There must be life in a world beyond this one, a world of reward and punishment. Justice is meted out in the next world. The only Biblical hint of this new idea is a single verse in the book of Daniel, a late addition to the canon which often deals with apocalyptic themes. "And many of those who sleep in the dust of the earth shall awake, some to everlasting life, and some to shame and everlasting contempt" (Daniel 12:2). This verse speaks of reward and punishment, but only after those asleep will wake up. It seems to refer to reward and punishment after a resurrection of the dead, an idea that will become vital in later religious thought.

Heaven and Hell

There is nothing in the Hebrew Bible about heaven and hell. These ideas will develop in later religious thought in each of the major Western religions, Judaism, Christianity, and Islam. Again, let me look at my own faith, Judaism. Where does the reward and punishment take place?

To Jews, heaven is the most beautiful place they could imagine, *Gan Eden* "The Garden of Eden." It is the place where the righteous will receive their justly earned reward. At a funeral, Jews recite a prayer for the dead called *El Malei Rahamim* "God full of Mercy." It includes the line, "May *Gan Eden* be their place of rest." It is the place of reward for the just.

To Jews, hell is the most horrible place they could imagine, a valley outside Jerusalem where the ancient Moabites used to sacrifice children. It is known as the valley of Hinam, *Gai Hinom*, or *Gehinnom*. The wicked are sent to *Gehinnom* to be purged of their impurities. But *Gehinnom* is different from the eternal damnation of Christianity, made famous by Dante. It is a place of temporary punishment, no more than a year. And there is no punishment on the Jewish Sabbath. After the soul is purged of its sins, it can enter *Gan Eden*.

Jews speak of *Gan Eden* and *Gehinnom*, but the ideas are deliberately vague. The emphasis is how to live in this world, not what will happen in the next. Our goal is to create heaven on earth rather than to get into heaven. That is why people say that Judaism, far more than other Western faiths, is this-worldly.

Let me share my own idea of *Gan Eden* and *Gehinnom,* one I developed from something I read from the Baal Shem Tov (1698-1760), the founder of Hasidism. Suppose we send one of our children to the store with instructions to buy certain goods. If our child does the task properly, she can gladly return to us, feeling good about what shat she accomplished. But if our child misspent that money and did not do the task properly, she would return home frightened to face our anger. Like that child, God sends us into this world to do certain tasks. If we do our best, we can comfortably face our Maker. That is *Gan Eden*. But if we avoid the task and live an improper life in this world, we face our Maker with fear and dread. That is *Gehinnom*.

Resurrection and Reincarnation

Gan Eden and *Gehinnom* are part of Jewish tradition, but they are not as fully developed as the ideas of heaven and hell in other Western religions. Perhaps part of the reason is that they are temporary abodes. Judaism has developed the idea of resurrection, that the soul will come back to the body. This idea already appears in the famous passage of Ezekiel's Valley of the Dry Bones (see Ezekiel, chapter 37). The prophet sees a valley filled with dry bones who soon are resurrected back to life. Judaism repeats this idea in the *Amidah*, the daily prayer recited several times a day by Jews.

Baruch Ata Adonai, Mechayei HaMetim, "Praised are You, O Lord, Who brings the dead to life."

Whether or not one takes the prayer literally or as a metaphor, it reflects a powerful idea. As human beings, our work is to be done in this material world. The dead cannot do good deeds or try to perfect the world. As the Psalmist said, "The dead cannot praise God, nor those who go down in silence" (Psalms 115:17). A soul needs to return to this world to continue its unfinished work. In fact, this idea is reflected in the Jewish idea that a body must be buried as undamaged as possible. The body must be ready for the moment when the soul reenters.

There is another approach to the soul returning to the body which can be found in Jewish mysticism. It is known as *gilgul* or *gilgulei neshamot,* the reincarnation of souls. The soul comes back once again to a new body to continue its work upon the earth. Although this idea can be found among the ancient Greek Pythagoreans, its source may be Eastern religions such as Hinduism and Buddhism. According to these traditions, the soul comes back to fulfill its *karma*, receiving its just reward or punishment for behavior in a previous life.

Nonetheless, there is a major difference between reincarnation in Eastern traditions and Jewish mysticism. In Eastern traditions, the goal is to escape the unending cycle of *samsara*, or the constant return of the soul to this world. The soul seeks to escape to a perfect place or *nirvana*. In Jewish mysticism, the soul seeks to return to this material world to continue its work. The goal is not to escape from this world but to embrace it. The material world is where the action is.

The deep lesson is that our soul takes on a body and enters the material world with a mission to perform. Nobody totally completes that mission in a lifetime. But we must still do the work when we are alive. The Talmud teaches, "Rabbi Tarfon said, It is not our duty to finish the task, nor are we free to avoid it altogether" (*Avot* 2:16). We do what we can in this world, then we return to continue our task. Judaism emphasizes the importance of the soul's work in this world, not in some spiritual realm.

Dualism, the idea of a material body and a spiritual soul, are central ideas in the Western religions of Judaism, Christianity and Islam. With an eternal soul that survives death, individual justice can prevail. The soul can receive its reward and punishment in the next world. It is an idea that pervades Western thought and gives great comfort to multitudes of people. If we suffer in this life, we will receive our just reward in the next. Those who are evil in this life will receive their just desserts in the next life. With this powerful idea, there is a sense of justice.

But ideas do not enter religions out of nowhere. In this case, the source of an eternal soul came from a different tradition altogether. It was borrowed from the Greeks, and particular, the great philosopher Plato (427–347 BCE).

Chapter 2
Trapped in a Cave: The Soul in Plato

One of the earliest thought experiments goes back to the pre-Socratic philosopher Zeno of Elea (495-430 BCE). Zeno tried to prove that the material world we live in is an illusion. He developed several paradoxes to show that motion is not real.

Perhaps Zeno's most famous paradox is Achilles and the Tortoise.[19] Suppose Achilles is running a race with a tortoise and, to be fair, he gives the tortoise a head start. When Achilles begins to run, the tortoise is ahead of him. When Achilles reaches that spot, the tortoise has moved further ahead. When Achilles reaches that spot, the tortoise again has moved ahead. So it will go on forever. Achilles could never catch the tortoise. Therefore, reality is an illusion.

One of my college students approached me before my Introduction to Philosophy class. He was surprised that I was teaching college philosophy. How can I be a rabbi and teach secular philosophy? Don't they contradict each other? After all, religion gets truth from revelation, sacred scripture, and properly ordained authority. Philosophy gets truth from open ended free debate. What could religion and philosophy have in common?

My student sounded like the early Church father Tertullian (155–220). He famously said, "What has Athens to do with Jerusalem?"[20] Athens is the birthplace of philosophy while Jerusalem is the center of religion. The two should have nothing to do with each other. Religion begins with faith while philosophy begins with arguments. How can I accept both?

I answered that it was a great question. I prefer the approach of the great Christian thinker considered a saint by the Catholic Church, Anselm of Canterbury (1033–1109). Anselm invented the ontological proof for the existence of God, which philosophers still argue over to this day. He defined philosophy as "faith seeking understanding."[21] Such religious thinkers as the Muslim Avicenna, the Jewish Maimonides, and the Christian Thomas Aquinas begin with faith, and use philosophical arguments to deepen their faith. Personally, my study of secular philosophy has deepened my Jewish faith.

In fact, the Rabbis of the Talmudic period had a surprising respect for the Greek philosophical tradition. In the Talmud (*Megillah* 9b), the sage Rabban Shimon ben Gamliel allows Torah scrolls to be written in Greek. He based this on the blessing in the Torah that Noah gives his sons. "God shall enlarge Japheth and he shall dwell in the tents of Shem" (Genesis 9:27). Japheth was the progenitor of *Yavan*, the Hebrew word for Greek. The Rabbis seem to read the verse from Genesis that the traditions of Greece shall enlighten the tent of the Hebrews.

We must now move to ancient Greece for our study of the soul. In particular, the thinker who gave this idea to the world was Plato. Plato was so influential that the modern philosopher Alfred North Whitehead (1861-1947), whom we will meet later in this book, said that the entire Western philosophical tradition is "a series of footnotes to Plato."[22] But before we can look at Plato, we must study the founder of the philosophical method, Plato's teacher Socrates. And before we can look at Socrates, we must study a famous debate between two pre-Socratic philosophers, Heraclitus and Parmenides.

Heraclitus and Parmenides

One of the oldest debates in philosophy asks the question, what is the root of our knowledge? (This is the branch of philosophy called epistemology or the theory of knowledge.) How do we know what we know? Does knowledge come from our senses, by looking out into the world? We call this approach to knowledge empiricism. Or does knowledge come through our mind, by thinking about the world? We call this approach to knowledge rationalism. The argument between the empiricists (knowledge comes through our senses) and the rationalists (knowledge comes from our mind) began in ancient Greece and continues to this very day.

One can say that Heraclitus (b. approximately 500 BCE) was the first empiricist. He looked out into a world that seemed to be constantly in flux. Movement and change were everywhere. He notably said, "You cannot step into the same river twice."[23] Every time one steps into a river, it is new water, the shape of the river may change, the temperature may change, and one becomes a slightly different person. We live in a world of constant change.

On the other hand, one can say Parmenides (b. 515 BCE) was the first rationalist. Rather than looking out into the world, he thought deeply about it. Change seems impossible, for change means something new must come out of nothing. He said, "What is, is. What is not, is not."[24] Change is an illusion. The Greek philosopher Zeno of Elea developed a series of paradoxes like Achilles and the tortoise to prove that change is impossible. Beneath the material world which seems to be constantly in flux, there must be an unchangeable reality.

In the argument between Heraclitus and Parmenides, we see the earliest confrontation between empiricism and rationalism. The empiricists see a world of constant flux, while the rationalists see a world without change. So who is correct? Plato would teach that they both are correct. There are two worlds. One is a world of change, growth, and decay. The other is an unchangeable world of perfect forms. With Plato, we see an early form of dualism. This material world is a changing world. But most important is a spiritual world of perfect, unchanging forms. This idea of a perfect spiritual world deeply influenced Western religions.

Plato's Teacher Socrates

Before looking at Plato in more detail, let us turn to Plato's teacher Socrates, the founder of the dialogues which are at the heart of philosophy. Socrates (470–399 BCE) never wrote anything himself. We know his position from the dialogues written about him, particularly by Plato. Socrates loved to go out into the marketplace and confront people with questions about the deepest ideas in human thought. What is justice? What is piety? What is virtue? Unfortunately, Socrates was sentenced to death by the citizens of Athens for corrupting the youth of the city. His argument about the existence of the soul after his death by drinking hemlock will become central to our argument for the existence of the soul.

Socrates' major argument was directed against a group of itinerant teachers of rhetoric known as the Sophists. The Sophists taught that there are no absolute truths. To quote one of the most famous, Protagoras (48– 411 BCE), "Man is the measure of all things."[25] There is no absolute truth, but rather, all truth is manmade. (The Sophist position is strangely similar to modern postmodernism which teaches that all truth is relative.) To understand the Sophists, perhaps it is best to imagine a modern attorney. He or she can passionately argue both sides of a case. A good attorney can argue for one client, then switch sides and argue with equal passion for another client. There are no absolute truths.

Socrates passionately disagreed with the Sophists. There is absolute truth. One can say that this truth exists in a perfect, unchanging world, which Plato would later call the World of the Forms. Justice may be imperfect in this material world, but there is a world of perfect justice. Beauty may be imperfect in this world, but there is a world of perfect beauty. We can reach that perfect world through rational argument. Socrates taught that "knowledge leads to virtue" [26] and "the unexamined life is not worth living." Our mind can reach this perfect, unchanging world. He would use perhaps the most famous thought experiment in philosophy: the Allegory of the Cave.[27]

The Allegory of the Cave

In his dialogue *The Republic*, Plato paints the image of prisoners in a cave. The prisoners are tied down so that they can only see a wall. On that wall are the shadows of objects. The prisoners cannot see the objects but only the shadows on the wall. They had been prisoners their entire lives, so their entire world consists of these shadows on the wall. For these prisoners, these shadows are the only reality.

Then one day a prisoner escapes and turns his back to the wall, for the first time seeing what is creating the images. At first, he only sees a bright light which blinds him. But then he sees objects moving in front of the light, casting shadows on the wall. He realizes that these objects are real, and the shadows on the wall are but images. There is a world of reality beyond what can be seen reflected on the wall.

The prisoner is so excited that he comes back to tell his fellow prisoners the truth about the images they see. But they do not believe him, and upset by what they learn, they eventually kill him. The prisoners would rather continue seeing the images on the wall than the true source of those images.

Of course, the prisoner who is killed for telling the truth is Socrates. The images on the wall represent the material world in which we live, a world full of change and decay, of imperfections. But this world is a mere reflection of a more perfect world, an unchangeable world which is casting its shadows. They are the unchangeable reality. The goal of life is to leave, at least with our minds, the imperfect World of Shadows and see the perfect World of the Forms. We can see them using what Plato called "the mind's eye."

Perhaps the best example to demonstrate the World of the Forms is mathematics, particularly geometry. In this imperfect world in which we live, we can draw shapes such as triangles and circles. But they will always be imperfect. No matter how sharp our tools or skilled our hands, we cannot draw an infinitely thin, infinitely straight line. Perfect triangles and circles do not exist in our material world. They only exist in the perfect World of the Forms. Shapes and even numbers in this world are mere reflections of that more perfect world.

Not only mathematical objects, but everything in this physical world is a shadow of something in a more perfect world. A horse in this world might become injured and will eventually die. Things of this world decay. A perfect horse exists only in the World of the Forms. Descriptions such as colors also exist in the World of the Forms. Adjectives such as strong or intelligent exist in this perfect world. Everything in this world is an inferior reflection of that perfection.

Finally, perfect ethical ideas exist only in the World of the Forms. Justice, piety, or virtue may exist in this world, but they are imperfect. They are merely reflections of perfect justice, perfect piety, or perfect virtue. How do we reach these perfections? Following Socrates, we reach them through our mind. This was Socrates' complaint against the Sophists, who believed that "man is the measure of all things."   Human values are man-made. To Socrates and his student Plato, perfect values only exist in a perfect spiritual world. We can reach them through our mind.

Trapped in the World

We humans exist in an imperfect world of sin and decay. But it is our bodies which are trapped in this world. We also come from a perfect World of the Forms. We came from there and one day we will return there. When I teach my Introduction to Philosophy college class, I ask my students, "Have you ever heard the idea that we come from a perfect place, we are thrown into this imperfect world, but do not worry, some day we will return to that perfect place?" When they answer yes, I ask where that idea comes from.

Most of them answer that they heard it in church, mosque, or synagogue, from a priest, minister, imam, or rabbi. They assume it comes from the Bible. I then reply, "The idea is not found in the Bible. It comes from Plato." The idea of the soul coming from a perfect spiritual world was a Greek contribution to Western thought.

To Plato, the soul comes from the perfect World of the Forms and will someday return there. In his dialogue *The Phaedo*[28], Plato uses Socrates as the spokesman to prove the existence of the immortal soul. The dialogue takes place on the day that Socrates drinks hemlock and ends his life. He tries to prove that he is at peace as he faces his demise, knowing that only his body will die. His soul will continue to live.

In the dialogue Socrates brings numerous proofs for the immortality of the soul. Let me mention my favorite proof, often called the *theory of recollection*. To Plato, knowledge is intrinsic to our minds and learning is simply remembering. In fact, in another dialogue Plato will show how a slave with no education was able to prove the Pythagorean Theorem simply using his mind, from information he recalled from before he was born. We are all born with inherent knowledge; learning is merely recalling what we already know. Where did this knowledge come from? Our souls knew it from our time in the World of the Forms before we were born.

Part of the reason I love this idea is that it fits with a lovely Rabbinic teaching (*Niddah* 30b). When we are in the womb, an angel teaches us the entire Torah, all knowledge we need to know before we go forth into the world. Then as we are ready to be born, the angel touches us above the lip, and we forget everything we learned. That is the reason we have a small indentation above our lip. The angel says, "Go out into the world and be good."   Jewish tradition teaches that we forget everything we learned. But deep in the recesses of our mind, this knowledge of everything still exists. According to this teaching, learning is recollection of what we already know.   Rationalists such as Socrates and Plato believe that humans are born with innate knowledge. To learn is to uncover that knowledge.

Perhaps the strongest proof from the Bible that humans are born with this innate knowledge is the story of Cain and Abel at the beginning of Genesis. Cain kills his brother Abel, and when confronted by God, replies, "Am I my brother's keeper?"   Cain already senses that he had done something wrong. God then punishes Cain, making him a wanderer on the earth. But at this point God had not yet given the prohibition against murder. That would only happen with the story of Noah, and later the Ten Commandments. Nonetheless, Cain was expected to know that murder was wrong. There are some things we humans know from birth.

Our mind is not a blank slate, a *tabula rasa* as the empiricist philosopher John Locke (1632-1704) would someday teach. We humans seem to have certain innate knowledge from before our birth. Plato teaches that knowledge is recollection, remembering what we knew before we were born into this world. And if one's soul exists before they take on a body, then one's soul exists after the body dies. Plato teaches that the soul is immortal.

From Athens to Jerusalem

How did an idea that came from Greek philosophy become a central tenet of Western tradition? How did Athens and Jerusalem come together? It is difficult to unravel completely the history of ideas and how they influence one another. But perhaps the most important thinker who combined the thought of Plato with early Christianity was one of the great fathers of the early Christianity, Augustine of Hippo (354–430), who Catholics know as Saint Augustine. He built a theology which is central to Christian thinking to this day, including ideas about the fall of man and original sin.

It is noteworthy to mention that earlier in his life, Augustine was a follower of Manichaeism. Manicheanism, considered by Christians as a great heresy, believes that there are two forces at work in the world, one good and one evil. Life is a clash between these two forces. This idea is still influential to this very day. Think about people who believe in a world of God versus Satan, or for *Star Wars* fans, the force versus the dark side. By pitting a force of evil against the force of good, Manicheanism explains the presence of suffering in the world.

When Augustine became a Christian, although he may have rejected the Manichean dualism of good and evil, he still accepted the dualism of Plato. The world was divided into body and soul. The soul was good, but the body was tainted with evil. The soul, which comes from a perfect place, must struggle with evil while entrapped within the body. It is corrupted by sin, with roots in the sin of Adam. Nonetheless, the sojourn of the soul in this material world is temporary. It will eventually return to the ideal World of the Forms. Many scholars have commented on how Augustine's theology reflects the Manicheanism of his younger days. Instead of a force of good and a force of evil, we now have a soul and a body. As Plato taught, the body is part of an imperfect physical world.

In general, Judaism did not accept this idea that the body and the material world is tainted with evil. After all, God looked at God's creation and saw that it was very good. Nonetheless, there were thinkers who attempted to combine Judaism with Plato's philosophy. Perhaps the most influential was Philo of Alexandria (20 BCE–50 CE) who lived several centuries before Augustine. To quote Philo, "For each of us has come into this world as into a foreign city, in which before our birth we had no part, and in this city he does sojourn, until he has exhausted his appointed span of life." [29]   A soul comes from a perfect place into this imperfect world, and then returns to that perfect place.

Where did this imperfect world, a place of decay and of sin, come from? Plato in his dialogue *Timaeus*,[30] teaches a creation story very different from Genesis. A creator called a demiurge, not the God of the Bible but an inferior being or lesser god, formed this world. The demiurge used the perfect forms and primordial matter to shape a material world. To the Greeks, this undifferentiated matter was called *hyle*. From this we get a key Platonic idea. Form can exist without matter. And matter can exist without form. The creation of the world is the combination of form and matter.

Now we can see the immense influence of Plato on Western religion. To the religious thinkers who built on Plato's philosophy, the soul is form and the body is matter. In the womb they come together. But at death they separate. The body deteriorates and becomes undifferentiated matter (*hyle*) once again. The soul returns to the perfect World of the Forms. Both form and matter can exist independently. Only in this world do they exist together, but this is temporary.

It will be Plato's student Aristotle who will challenge his teacher. To Aristotle, form cannot exist without matter and matter cannot exist without form. Aristotle would develop a totally different view of reality, one far closer to empiricism (knowledge comes from the senses) than rationalism (knowledge comes from the mind.) Until the seventeenth century, the philosophy of Aristotle was considered authoritative throughout the West. What did Aristotle say about the soul?

Chapter 3

The Great Chain of Being: The Soul in Aristotle

One of the earliest thought experiments from the Enlightenment was Galileo's proof that Aristotle was wrong. Aristotle taught that heavy items fall to earth faster than lighter items. Galileo sought to challenge the scientific outlook of his age, which was based on Aristotle. Tradition says that he proved that all items fall at the same speed by dropping objects off the Leaning Tower of Pisa.

He also proved it through a thought experiment. Imagine a heavy object and a light object tied together. The light object would fall more slowly, retarding the speed of the two falling together. But then the two falling together weigh more so they should fall faster. There is a contradiction, which shows that Aristotle was wrong. All objects fall at the same rate, at least in a vacuum. One of the results of the scientific revolution was to overturn Aristotle's entire science, that all items move according to inner drives or final causes.[31]

Between 1510 and 1511, the Italian Renaissance painter Raphael painted his famous fresco *The School of Athens* (*Scuola di Atene*). The painting adorns the walls of the Stanze di Raffaello in the Apostolic Palace in the Vatican. At the center of the painting are images of the two great Greek philosophers, Plato and Aristotle, in dispute. The older man Plato is pointing towards the sky. The younger man Aristotle is pointing towards the ground. This illustrates the fundamental disagreement between the two philosophers on the ultimate nature of reality. Is reality found beyond this world, in an ideal World of the Forms, as Plato taught? Or is reality rooted in this world of material objects, as Aristotle taught?

If Plato was a rationalist, his student Aristotle was an empiricist. Knowledge comes from the senses. In fact, he said, "There is nothing in the mind that is not first in the senses."[32] One could say that he was one of the first scientists of history. He loved studying nature. He was also a brilliant prolific writer, who wrote about everything from physics to metaphysics and from politics to logic. In fact, he invented logic. Before we can turn to Aristotle's view of the soul, we must summarize how he viewed the empirical world he studied.

Substance Ontology

Aristotle lived in a world of substances. We sometimes call his approach *substance ontology*. (The word "ontology" means the study of what exists. To Aristotle, only substances exist.) It was a world of material objects rather than spiritual forms. In fact, there could not be form without matter. The term used for Aristotle's approach is hylomorphism. We already saw the word *hyle* refers to matter. *Morphos* refers to form or shape. In modern English we say that one shape morphs into another. For Aristotle, form can also refer to function, how things work. Hylomorphism says that matter and form must always go together, there is no matter without form and no form without matter. On this issue, Aristotle broke with his teacher Plato.

Aristotle taught that every substance has four attributes, what he called the four causes. These are the material cause, the formal cause, the efficient cause, and the final cause. First there is the material cause, the matter of which it is made. For example, a statue in the park of a Roman general might be made of marble. But it also has a formal cause, its shape or function. It may appear to be a general on horseback holding a sword. The matter and form go together.

In addition, everything has an efficient cause. This is the cause that brought it into existence. How did it come into being? In the case of the statue, the efficient cause is the sculptor. Every substance in the world has an efficient cause, something that brought it into existence. Also, according to Aristotle, there cannot exist an infinite chain of such efficient causes. There must be a first cause, something that began the whole process, or to use the words of philosophers, something that was *necessary* rather than *contingent*. Aristotle called that first cause the unmoved mover. Later, religious interpreters of Aristotle such as Maimonides and Thomas Aquinas would use the idea of an unmoved mover to prove the existence of God.

Perhaps the most important idea in Aristotle's philosophy is the presence of a final cause in every substance. Every object in the universe has a final cause, a reason why it came into existence. The statue came into existence to honor a Roman general. Everything has a reason why it exists, and everything moves in order to fulfill its purpose. Aristotle believed in teleology, everything has a *telos* – a purpose or goal. Aristotle's physics sees all motion as attempts of substances to fulfill their purpose. For example, a rock will seek to move towards the ground where it belongs. And as mentioned above, according to Aristotle a heavier rock would move faster. It would take almost two millennia for Galileo to prove Aristotle wrong. The scientific revolution which began in the Renaissance overturned Aristotelian physics which had existed for almost two millennia.

According to Aristotle's view, the sun, the moon, and the five planets known at that time move in perfect circles around the earth because that is their purpose. As we mentioned, rocks fall to the earth because that is where they belong. Fire moves toward the sky because that is where it belongs. All material things consist of various combinations of earth, water, air, and fire. Each moves according to a self-directed teleology. This is how the West understood motion for thousands of years, until it was undermined by the scientific thinking of Copernicus, Kepler, Galileo, and Newton. The new science taught that movement was based on forces such as gravity, not inner desires. Modernity may have overturned Aristotle, but only after great conflict.

The Soul in Aristotle

All living things seek to fulfill their final purpose. Aristotle wrote a treatise on the soul called *De Anima*.[33] In the book, he identified the body of all living things with the material cause and the soul with the formal cause. As mentioned above, the formal cause can also be the function of a substance. One could say that Aristotle saw the soul as the function of all living things, that inner drive which gave it life. The soul was not a separate entity that exists independently of the body. To Aristotle, just as you cannot have a form without matter, you cannot have a soul without a body. Aristotle rejected the dualist view taught not only by Plato, but by the Western Abrahamic faiths.

Aristotle saw different living things as having various levels of the soul. Thus, he introduces an idea which will become central to medieval Christianity: The Great Chain of Being. At the bottom of the chain are plants. Their souls seek nutrition, growth, and reproduction.   The souls of plants do not need to have consciousness. They simply need to function in a way that causes the plant to fulfill its purpose. To Aristotle, the soul is the spirit of life within a living thing, We mentioned earlier that the philosopher Henri Bergson would later call this the *Élan Vital*.

Higher up on the great chain of being are animals, with higher animals having more developed souls than lower animals. In addition to nutrition, growth, and reproduction, animals also experience movement and sensation. They can feel pleasure and pain. They search for food, seek to reproduce, and flee from danger. This allows each animal to fulfill its purpose in the world.

The highest level of the soul is that of humanity. It shares everything with plants and animals, but it is also a rational soul. The ability to reason makes humans unique. Humans can "consider what their purpose is and choose to fulfill it. Aristotle defined human purpose with a fancy Greek word, *eudemonia,* often translated as "pleasure" but a word meaning "fulfillment." Humans satisfy their purpose by striving to live a life of fulfillment. This is achieved by practicing virtue. In his book *The Nichomachean Ethics*[34], Aristotle built an entire ethical system on the need of the rational soul to seek fulfillment. His system is called virtue ethics, and it is one of the great ethical systems in Western philosophy. Philosophers who teach ethics will often compare and contrast three systems: Aristotle's virtue ethics, Jeremy Bentham's utilitarianism, and Immanuel Kant's deontology.

To Aristotle plants, animals, and human beings all have souls. The soul is what animates the body, allowing it to function. Based on this description of Aristotle's position, the soul needs a body just as the body needs a soul. It seems that when the body dies, the soul also dies. There is no eternal soul. This is very similar to the original Biblical view of the soul as *nefesh*, the spirit which animates the body. In the Bible, when the body dies, that spirit returns to God. It has no independent existence. As we mentioned earlier, the body and soul are like the hardware and the software of a computer; neither can function without the other.

Nonetheless, medieval philosophy by Muslims, Jews, and Christians attempted to fuse religion with Aristotle. The Muslim Avicenna, the Jewish Maimonides, and the Christian Thomas Aquinas built entire philosophical systems by reconciling their faith with Aristotle. To Maimonides, he was simply "The Philosopher." The entire system of scholasticism, universally taught in European universities through the sixteenth century was a combination of Christianity and Aristotle's philosophy. How could this religious faith be reconciled with a pagan philosopher who did not believe in an eternal soul?

The Active Intellect

Part of the solution to the existence of an eternal soul lies in Aristotle's own writing. It is found in a section of Aristotle's book on the soul, *De Anima*, that is extremely difficult and open to interpretation. Let us try to unravel what Aristotle writes.

Aristotle speaks of the highest part of the human soul as the active intellect, also sometimes called the agent intellect. The rational part of the human soul is divided into two parts, the passive intellect and the active intellect. The passive intellect is all the potential knowledge that the mind can use in cognition. It consists of memories, sensations, and emotions. But it only exists in potential. This passive information needs some active agent to make it accessible. This became the role of the active intellect.

The active intellect is the part of the mind which processes this potential input and comes up with rational thought. It is like the Central Processing Unit (CPU) of a computer. It receives the intellectual forms of things and makes potential knowledge into actual knowledge. It is the active intellect which is at the heart of the human soul. Aristotle compares it to light which makes colors come to life.

According to Aristotle (he is somewhat vague about this), the active intellect is eternal and indestructible. All the other parts of the soul which we have discussed - the drive for growth, nutrition, reproduction, sensation, and movement - die when the body dies. Even the passive intellect dies when the body dies. But the active intellect exists at a higher level, in a dimension beyond the material. Aristotle compared it to the unmoved mover, which for the pagan Aristotle can be compared to God. In other words, the human soul, by its rational nature, contains a part of God within it.

Alexander of Aphrodesias (the early commentator on Aristotle born mid-second century BCE) taught that this active intellect was external to the human mind.[35] Because it has access to a fixed and stable set of human concepts, it must be linked to some central store of knowledge. It must be part of something universal and unchangeable. A theist could interpret the active intellect as being part of God. It is as if part of a universal soul is in each individual human. Even if the rest of the soul dies with the body, this part survives.

This was the opening used by medieval Islamic, Jewish, and Christian philosophers to combine their respective religions with Aristotle. To illustrate, in his master work *A Guide for the Perplexed*, Maimonides (1138-1204) built on the idea of the active intellect to explain God's gift of prophecy. Humans have a part of God within them.

Let us briefly describe Maimonides' philosophy. Maimonides ends his Guide with a famous allegory. Imagine a palace with people seeking to reach the king. Some people have their backs to the palace. They never strive for any knowledge at all. Some people walk around outside but never find the door. Those who wonder around outside but never enter the palace are pious Jews who observe commandments but never seek God intellectually. Some people enter but never get close to the king. Those who study some subjects like mathematics can enter the palace. But only a few people make it into the king's presence. These are the true philosophers who study God at the highest level. These are the people whose souls survive.[36]

For Maimonides, the vegetable and animal parts of the soul die with the body. Only the highest intellectual part continues to exist after death. But it continues by becoming at one with God. The part of us that contemplates God, the act of contemplation, and the object of contemplation become one. It is a confusing idea. Imagine the intellect like the breath that returns to God. To quote his *Guide for the Perplexed*:

> It must now be obvious to you that whenever the intellect is found in action, the intellect and the thing comprehended are one and the same thing; and also that the function of all intellect, namely, the act of comprehending, is its essence. The intellect, that which comprehends and that which is

comprehended, are therefore the same, whenever a real comprehension takes place.[37]

For Maimonides, the highest level of the soul survives death not simply because it contemplates God. It survives because it is part of God which dwells in each of us. He would use the Hebrew word *shefa*, literally "overflow," a flow of God into the human rational mind. To quote Maimonides again, "Prophecy is, in truth and reality, an emanation sent forth by the Divine Being through the medium of the Active Intellect, in the first instance to man's rational faculty, and then to his imaginative faculty."[38]

Maimonides' interpretation allows for a part of the soul that survives death. But it is far from the individual entity, still conscious, dwelling in *HaOlam HaBa* or the World to Come. It is closer to a divine breath in each of us that is part of the divinity. Although Maimonides spent his life fighting Jewish mysticism, we will later see that this is extremely close to the mystical view of the soul.

The Scientific Revolution

The dawn of the scientific revolution in the sixteenth century saw the end of Aristotle's influence. Copernicus taught that the sun, not the earth, was at the center of the universe, with the earth going around the sun. Kepler taught that planets moved in ellipses rather than circles. Galileo saw the heavens as imperfect, that other planets had moons and the sun had spots. Like Copernicus, he also taught a heliocentric view of the universe. For this he was kept under house arrest by the Catholic Church for the remainder of his life.

It was Isaac Newton who finally overturned Aristotle once and for all with his laws of motion and his theory of gravity. To quote the poet Alexander Pope (1688–1744),

Nature and Nature's laws lay hid in night;
God said, Let Newton be! And all was light.[39]

Substances did not move according to inner forces, seeking to fulfill their final purpose. There was no teleology in the universe. Large objects did not fall faster than small objects. Rather, there were strict scientific laws, written in the language of mathematics, that could describe the movement of everything from objects on earth to the planets. Aristotle's ideas, having explained the world for almost two millennia, were now dead. No one could imagine that today; some thinkers are starting to rethink Aristotle. But we will return to that later in this book.

For the moment, with the classical Aristotelean understanding of the world challenged by modern science, there had to be a new way to understand the world. It would take a new thinker, doubting all the wisdom from the past, to develop a new philosophy. René Descartes became the father of modern philosophy. It was Descartes who would take the dualism of the Bible and Plato and use it to develop a new way of understanding the world. With that, he developed the system named after him, known as Cartesian dualism.

Chapter 4
The Ghost in the Machine: The Soul in Descartes

A modern thought experiment was conceived by Harvard philosopher Robert Nozick (1938-2002) in his 1974 book Anarchy, State, and Utopia[40] called The Experience Machine or the Pleasure Machine. It was an attack on contemporary hedonism.

Suppose you could be hooked up to a machine that would give you non-stop pleasure all the time. There would be no pain, just joyous sensations. Nozick claimed that most of us would refuse such a machine. We would prefer to live in the real world, even with its pains. Nozick taught that human beings prefer actual reality to virtual reality.

René Descartes (1596–1650) is considered the father of modern philosophy. He is also the most prominent philosophical dualist. In fact, philosophers use the phrase "Cartesian dualism" to refer to the belief in two separate substances, mind and matter.

Descartes was the right man born at the right time. As mentioned in the previous chapter, the scientific revolution had overturned Aristotelian physics: that all substances move to fulfill their final cause. Teleology had been removed from the universe. To add to the confusion of the age, the religious authority of the

Catholic Church was under attack. Martin Luther (1483-1546) had nailed his 95 theses to the door of the Wittenberg Church, challenging fundamental Catholic beliefs and practices. Europe would be thrust into centuries of war and conflict between Catholics and Protestants. Of course, during these events, in addition to Christians of various beliefs, there were Jewish and Muslim communities in Europe. Where could one turn for authoritative truth?

Radical Skepticism

Descartes, although raised in France and a believing Catholic, was searching for a foundation for all knowledge which was beyond all doubt. He was a rationalist who believed that all knowledge comes through the mind. He could not trust the senses. After all, the senses can trick us; think about the way a pencil appears to be bent in a glass of water. We could even be dreaming. How do we know what is a dream and what is reality? One thinks of the classic Chinese philosopher Zhuangzi's (369–286 BCE) famous dream.[41] He dreamt he was a butterfly. When he awoke, he did not know if he was Zhuangzi dreaming he was a butterfly, or a butterfly dreaming he was Zhuangzi. Today we can also imagine Nozick's thought experiment. Could we be hooked up to a pleasure machine? What is reality?

Descartes decided to develop a method to achieve absolute knowledge. He began with radical skepticism. He doubted everything; all the authoritative tradition he had been taught. He doubted the existence of his own body. Perhaps he was being tricked by an evil demon (as we shall see, philosophers love demons.) Various philosophers have developed his Descartes idea of an evil demon into provocative thought experiments. Philosopher Gibert Harman (1938–2021) wrote of the "Brain in a Vat,"[42] where our brains do not perceive a real world but are hooked up by a mad scientist to chemicals which feed it information. Descartes' image became the basis of the popular *Matrix* movie series, where people are wired to a computer simulation. Today with the growth of virtual reality, the border between perception and reality is open to doubt. Descartes went so far as doubting all mathematical knowledge. Maybe this was also the work of an evil demon.

If everything is open to doubt, is there anything that one can say is true beyond doubt? Here Descartes came up with his famous *cogito*, perhaps the most famous statement in philosophy. *Cogito ergo sum*: "I think therefore I am." He could doubt everything except the fact that he was doubting, and by doubting, he was thinking. He was a thinking being. He had a mind. (Of course, later philosophers would attack Descartes. They would claim that he never proved he had a mind, simply that thinking exists. But we will ignore that objection.) To Descartes, it was a clear and distinct realization that he had a mind. The mind was a *res cogitans,* "a thinking thing." It did not take up space and was not divisible. Here Descartes introduces an idea regarding mind that will be vital as we continue this book – non-locality. Things located in space can be divided up. Since the mind cannot be divided, it is not located in any particular space.

A similar idea about the existence of a mind separate from the body was developed by the Islamic philosopher Avicenna (Ibn Sina 980–1037) hundreds of years before Descartes. He imagined a Floating Man,[43] who has never had contact with any physical objects. His world was suspended in the air. Nonetheless, he would have a mind and realize that he exists, even with no contact with the physical world. Avicenna was trying to prove the existence of the soul, but he demonstrated the idea that we have a mind.

Building All Knowledge

Descartes' *cogito* was simply the first step in building up all knowledge. His next step was to prove the existence of God. In his mind, he had the idea of God as a Being with all perfections. Something must have placed that idea in his mind. Such a Being must exist, for to lack existence is to lack perfection. In his demonstration that God exists, Descartes is using an argument introduced much earlier by Anselm of Canterbury (1033–1109). This is known as the ontological proof for the existence of God. It is proof based on the very definition of God. God, by definition, contains all perfections. Since existence is a perfection, God must exist. Philosophers continue to argue about the ontological proof of God to this day. Kurt Gödel (1906–1978), perhaps the greatest logician of the twentieth century, developed his own version of the ontological proof of God. We will look at Gödel's work later in this book.

Descartes had now proven that his mind exists, and that God exists. His next step was to prove that his body exists; in fact, that the entire material world exists. By definition, God is benevolent, absolutely good. A good God would not allow an evil demon to trick him. There is no evil demon; rather, the material world must really exist. A good God is proof that his perception of the world is accurate. But the material world is essentially different from the mental world.

Matter is *res extensa*, an extended thing. It takes up physical space. Since matter fills physical space, it can be divided. Matter which is *res extensa* is a totally different substance from mind, which is *res cogitans*. The world consists of two very different substances, thinking substances and extended substances. Since matter exists as a separate substance, it can be studied according to the scientific method developed by Francis Bacon (1561-1626) and others. Science is the study of matter, but mind is outside the purview of science. Mind is a totally separate entity with its own qualities.

Of course, we all know that matter and mind are not totally separate. They interact with one another. Our mind says to raise our arm and our body reacts, raising it. Our body is injured, and our mind feels pain. How could these two separate substances interact with one another? Descartes believed that this interaction takes place in the pineal gland, a gland whose purpose was not understood in Descartes' day. Today we know that the pineal gland secretes the hormone melatonin. The biggest problem with dualism in general and with Descartes' philosophy is - how can these two very different substances interact? How can mind affect matter and matter affect mind?

There is one other important point regarding Descartes. In his heart, he remained a devout Catholic. Humans have an eternal soul, but animals do not. The dualism of body and mind only applies to humans. To Descartes, animals do not have a mind; they are like automatons, mindless robots. Even in his own age, many people did not accept his view that animals do not have minds. Today, anyone who owns a dog or cat will testify that their pet has consciousness, perhaps not at a human level, but real, nonetheless.

Even if Descartes were wrong on the issue of animals, he gave a description of the universe that is shared by most people in the West. It is a description that agrees with the great Western religions and with the great philosopher Plato. Reality is made up of two different substances, bodies and minds or material and spiritual. Somehow these materials influence one another and interact. But both exist.

Descartes would be challenged by most scientists and philosophers to our own day. But one of the first to challenge him was a young woman who carried on a long correspondence with the philosopher. In an age when women's education was limited and women did not become philosophers, Princess Elisabeth of Bavaria challenged Descartes in a series of letters.

Princess Elisabeth of Bavaria

Princess Elisabeth of Bavaria (1618–1680) met Descartes as a young woman while on a trip to the Hague in the Netherlands. They began a correspondence which would continue through the remainder of Descartes' life.[44] He had the highest respect for her intellect and even dedicated one of his books to her. But he was never able to clearly answer her challenge to his substance dualism.

The essence of Elisabeth's problem with Descartes was the question of how a spiritual substance can move a material substance. According to Descartes, material objects take up space. According to the science of Descartes' day, such objects can only be moved through physical contact with other material objects. (Einstein's "spooky action at a distance" would not appear until centuries later.) Elisabeth asked, how could an object which has no physical substance and takes up no physical space cause a physical object to move? How could an immaterial soul move a material body? Descartes struggled to answer the young woman but never found a satisfactory answer.

Elisabeth's question can be translated today into modern science. One of the fundamental laws of the universe is the first law of thermodynamics. Energy can change form but cannot be created or destroyed. Today, with Einstein's discovery that matter is the equivalent of energy ($E=mc^2$), we can say that matter-energy cannot be created nor destroyed. Given a closed system, the amount of matter-energy is constant. Although it is open to debate, most physicists believe that the universe is a closed system. How can a spiritual substance such as a soul add energy by moving an object within a closed system? For that matter, if God is a spiritual substance, how can God move the matter within a closed system? How could divine providence possibly work?

The religious philosopher Alvin Plantinga (b. 1932) has offered a solution. He claims that the universe is not a closed system, but rather God is part of the system. God is allowed to intervene because God is within the system. To quote Plantinga,

> According to Newton and classical mechanics, natural laws describe how the world works when, or provided that the world is a closed (isolated) system, subject to no outside causal influence. In classical physics, the great conservation laws deduced from Newton's laws are stated for closed or isolated systems. These principles, therefore, apply to isolated or closed systems. If so, however, there is nothing in them to prevent God from changing the velocity or direction of a particle. If he did so, obviously, energy would not be conserved in the system in question; but equally obviously, that system would not be closed, in which case the principle of conservation of energy would not apply to it.[45]

Plantinga gives an intriguing answer, but it is not science. Scientific theories study the material world and leave no room for supernatural agency. So, Elisabeth's question remains, how could a totally spiritual substance move a material substance?

One answer given by many scientists is that mind or consciousness or a soul cannot affect the material world   They use the term epiphenomenon, something that appears as a result of a natural process but can never affect that natural process. It is simply a byproduct with no causal affect. It is like the plume of smoke that appears out of the engines of a jet plane; it exists but cannot affect the plane. I prefer the metaphor of the picture created by a television set. The picture is an epiphenomenon. It is created by a material object (the television set) but it cannot affect that object. A hand cannot reach out from the picture and turn off the television.

Epiphenomenalism is a challenge to the Cartesian substance dualism. Material causes can create mental events. But mental events cannot affect material causes. It is a one-way street, the precise opposite of what Descartes imagined. Princess Elisabeth has raised a profound challenge to Descartes. But other thinkers would go still further, attempting to undermine dualism all together.

Gilbert Ryle Challenges Descartes

British philosopher Gilbert Ryle (1900–1976) considered dualism to be a categorical mistake. He used the wonderful image of the *Ghost in the Machine*. [46] His image makes fun of Descartes' classical description of the body as a material object and the soul as a spiritual object, a ghost in a machine. To Ryle, Descartes was describing two separate substances, but according to Ryle, the two items are the same.

Being British, he imagined a tourist walking through Oxford University. Such a tourist would look at all the individual buildings, these are classrooms, these are labs, this is a dorm. Then the tourist asks the question, "This is nice, but where is the university?" The university is not something separate from the buildings that make up the university. That is the categorical mistake. So too, the mind is not something different from the matter that makes up the mind. All is one. Mind and matter are part of the same material substance.

So we come to the second metaphysical approach to reality – materialism. Perhaps we live in a world where everything is matter. This is the view of most modern philosophers and scientists. The universe consists of inert bits of matter moving through space according to the physical laws set forth by Isaac Newton. Let us turn our attention to materialism.

Part 2: Materialism

The French mathematician astronomer Pierre-Simon Laplace (1749–1827) developed a famous thought experiment known as Laplace's Demon.[47] (As mentioned earlier, philosophers love demons.) He imagined a demon with superior intelligence, who knew the location and motion of every particle of the universe. With such complete information, the demon could predict the future of every particle. The entire future of the universe could be known. He also taught that such a demon could retrodict (reconstruct the past) of every particle of the universe. The demon would know the entire past.

To Laplace, we live in an entirely material universe with absolute determination. The universe is simply a collection of particles moving according to the laws of nature. There is no room for any supernatural forces, anything working outside of nature. Even the human brain is strictly determined by the laws of nature. There is no eternal soul, and for Laplace, no room for God in such a universe. There is also no free will.

According to one possibly apocryphal story, Laplace gave a copy of his book *Celestial Mechanics* to Napoleon. Napoleon told Laplace that he saw no mention of God in his book. Laplace famously responded, "I have no need for that hypothesis."[48] With Laplace and other thinkers such as Thomas Hobbes, Julian Offray de La Mettrie, and centuries later, Karl Marx, materialism entered the world. The universe is simply matter in motion according to inexorable laws. Science is the study of those laws. The more we learn about science, the more we can predict all motion in the universe. There is no room for any supernatural intervention in nature, whether by individual souls or by God.

In the beginning, many Enlightenment thinkers became deists. Deism is the belief that God set the universe in motion and created the physical laws, but God does not intervene. In deism there are no miracles, no revelation, and no answer for prayers. God is the Creator who ever since, has ignored creation. Perhaps one of the most famous deists was Thomas Jefferson (1743–1826), author of the American Declaration of Independence. Jefferson prepared a Bible, known as the Jefferson Bible, keeping all the ethical teachings but removing any references to revelation and miracles.

Over time deism gave way to atheism among many (but not all) philosophers and scientists. Why posit a belief in God at all? The universe simply happened. The universe is matter in motion. Our job is to study the universe to understand its physical laws, without any speculation regarding spiritual matters. In fact, there was a group of thinkers in the mid-twentieth century known as the Vienna Circle, practicing what was called logical empiricism. They claimed that we can speak of only two matters: we can speak of the laws of logic, and we can speak of empirical or scientific facts. But to speak of anything else – religion, metaphysics, ethics, aesthetics

– is nonsense. To quote one of the great philosophical minds of the twentieth century Ludwig Wittgenstein (1889–1951), "Whereof one cannot speak, thereof one must be silent."[49] It was materialism at its most extreme. (Later we will return to Wittgenstein, who will reject this extreme materialism for a new philosophy.)

Materialism is often called physicalism, the idea that only physical substances exist. Of course, there is an obvious problem with materialism or physicalism. If the universe is just matter in motion, where does consciousness come from? How does a brain, a massive collection of billions of nerve cells, create a mind? What is a mind according to a materialist conception of the universe?

We will look at three answers given by materialists. Each can give us insights about consciousness, but each also raises problems. The three approaches are behaviorism, mind-brain identity theory, and functionalism. Let us study each of them.

Chapter 5
Philosophical Zombies: Behaviorism

Rava created a person and sent it before Rav Zeira.   Rav Zeira spoke to it, but it wouldn't reply. Rav Zeira said to it, you are a creation of one of my colleagues, return to your dust. Rav Hanina and Rav Ushaya would sit all of Erev Shabbat, occupied with a Book of Creation, and create for themselves a third-grown calf, and they would eat it. (Talmud Sanhedrin 65b)

Before exploring the materialistic view known as behaviorism, let us turn to the thinking of a prominent philosopher of mind who rejected materialism in favor of dualism. The Australian philosopher David Chalmers gave us the concept of *the hard problem of consciousness,* mentioned in the Introduction. We can study how some aspects of the mind work like perception, memory, and cognition. These are the soft problems of consciousness. But how do we explain subjective awareness? How do we explain how the mind sees colors, hears music, smells coffee, tastes ice cream, or feels a kitten's fur? This subjective awareness is *the hard problem of consciousness.*

Bodies Without Minds

Chalmers gives us a famous thought experiment to prove that the mind is not simply something physical. He introduces Philosophical Zombies. Philosophical Zombies are not like the zombies in the movies; they do not try to kill you and eat your brains. They are far more interesting. A philosophical zombie is a creature who looks and acts like a human in every way, except it has no consciousness. If you prick a philosophical zombie with a pin, it will flinch and say "ouch." But there is no inner awareness of pain. In fact, there is no inner awareness of anything. It looks and acts like a human without any subjective awareness. It has a complete human body with no mind.

Let us look at Chalmer's argument. It is part of philosophy known as modality, that which we can conceive as possible in some possible universe. Can I imagine an alternative universe where there is an exact physical copy of me, cell by cell, only with blue eyes instead of my brown eyes? The answer is that such a universe is impossible. If the copy of me matches me cell by cell, my copy must have the same-colored eyes. But can I imagine an alternative universe where there is an exact physical copy of me, cell by cell, only with no consciousness. It would have my body but no inner mind. Chalmers claims that such a universe is logically possible, at least in our imagination. If so, then consciousness must be something different from the material cells of my body. Consciousness or mind is non-material.

Many philosophers have challenged Chalmer's argument. But Chalmers insists that consciousness is something separate from the material of the universe. In fact, just as there are fundamental building blocks of matter such as quarks and electrons, so there must be fundamental building blocks of mind. According to Chalmers, mind is not an emergent property that requires complicated connections of brain cells. Rather, consciousness is one of these building blocks of the universe.

To explain Chalmers' view of mind, I sometimes like to use a humorous story. A speaker tells his audience that the world is on the back of a turtle. A woman interrupts, "What is the turtle standing on?" The speaker replies that the turtle is on the back of another turtle. The woman interrupts again, "What is that turtle standing on?" The frustrated speaker replies, "Madam, it is turtles all the way down." (The popular young adult novelist John Green [b. 1977] wrote a novel based on this story called *Turtles All the Way Down*.[50]) I imagine Chalmers answering in a similar way, "It is mind all the way down." The universe is built out of bits of mind.

We will return to this issue of bits of mind in the last section of this book when we speak of idealism. But meanwhile, we can use the idea of Philosophical Zombies to study behaviorism.

Behaviorism

Behaviorism teaches that we cannot speak of inner mental states because we cannot see such inner mental states. We can only speak of what we can perceive with our senses. And our senses can only see behavior. Therefore, mind can only be described by behavior. If we want to speak about feeling pain, we must describe the behavior of someone feeling pain – flinching or saying "ouch." All mental states are simply ways to describe certain behaviors. Mental states only exist as physical states, aspects of behavior.

Behaviorism grew out of psychology, particularly the work of people like Ivan Pavlov (1849–1936) and B.F. Skinner (1904–1990). Most of us have learned about Pavlov's experiments on dogs, how ringing a bell while feeding them caused the dogs to salivate. Soon the dogs were salivating whenever the bell was rung, even if there was no food. Behaviorism assumes the mind is like a black box, unknowable, but reacting to certain stimuli with certain responses. Skinner's work taught how certain behaviors could be motivated in a patient through certain stimuli, without concern for the inner mental state of the patient.

In philosophy of mind, behaviorism can be described by Chalmer's Philosophical Zombies. It is as if subjective mental states do not exist. Mind is defined by behavior only. The mental thought "I think it is going to rain" is defined by the physical action of carrying an umbrella. Behaviorism fits the scientific age. After all, we can see and measure a person's outer behavior. We have no way of seeing or measuring their inner subjective state. Science studies what we can measure and observe, and we cannot measure and observe inner subjective states.

In fact, how do we know that people even have inner subjective states? Maybe the people we meet are Philosophical Zombies, acting as if they are human but with no consciousness. There is a philosophical term called solipsism, which says that only my own mind exists. I know I have a mind, but how do I know if anybody else has one? Descartes taught that *I think therefore I am*. But Descartes' theory never addressed whether anyone else thinks or other minds exist. The main objection to solipsism is by analogy; I have a mind, other people look and act like me, so it makes sense that other people must also have minds. But analogy is a very weak source of information. We see our minds, but we only see other people's behavior.

Super Spartans

In truth, most of us accept the fact that Philosophical Zombies do not exist. Even Chalmers speaks about them in some other possible world. And most of us are not solipsists. Just as we have minds, we live our lives based on the acceptance of the existence of other minds. But the philosophy known as behaviorism persists among many philosophers and psychologists. There are people who believe that we can only speak of what we can see and measure. We can see behavior, but we cannot see other minds. It is easy to build a scientific theory based on the notion that people do not have inner, subjective experiences. Science deals with the objective, not the subjective.

American philosopher Hilary Putnam (1926–2016), whose name will come up again in this book, brings a fascinating challenge to behaviorism. What about people who have trained themselves so that their behavior does not match their inner subjective state. He imagined a group of what he called Super Spartans.[51] These are people who can withstand pain with no outer reaction. They feel the pain, even great pain. But they do not flinch, say ouch, or react in any other way. No observer could ever know they feel pain. One might call them super stoics. To Putnam, this proves that inner consciousness is different from outer behavior. As we shall see, he will eventually suggest an alternative theory for reconciling consciousness with a material universe.

The Turing Test

Let us not yet leave the issue of Philosophical Zombies. Could we create a machine that looks and acts like a human, that seems conscious, but lacks any inner subjective awareness? This was the problem posed by one of the great minds of the 20th century, Alan Turing (1912–1954). To learn about Turing's life, I strongly recommend the 2014 movie *The Imitation Game.*[52] It tells the true story of how Turing, a British subject and a brilliant mathematician, broke the Nazi's secret Enigma Code. Sadly, Turing lived in a less tolerant age and after World War II, was arrested for homosexuality. He lost his security clearance and eventually committed suicide.

.   In a sense, Turing also invented the computer. He conceived a theoretical machine with an infinitely long paper tape, with various characters written on that tape. There are rules that would apply for whatever character shows up on a tape. If the machine is in a particular state and a particular character shows up on the tape, the machine performs a particular action. The rules are precise. For example, if the machine is in state p and an a shows up on the tape, the machine would switch to state q and move the tape one space to the right. The Turing machine works using an algorithm, exact rules on what to do based on the input from the tape. This became the theoretical basis for the modern computer, which is simply a non-infinite Turing machine.   Computers work using algorithms to create a particular output, given a particular input.

Suppose we could build a machine, a computer or robot or even some kind of android, which could imitate the action of a human. Turing conceived a test of the intelligence of such a machine. Imagine a person feeding questions to either a human being or a machine located behind a closed door. The person feeding the questions has no knowledge whether a human being or a machine is answering the questions. If after a certain amount of time, the person feeding the questions cannot tell if a person or a machine is responding, then for all intents and purposes, the machine is a person.[53] A machine that passes the Turing test can be considered a person with consciousness. Today regular contests are held to see if someone can develop a machine that would pass the Turing test. There is an annual contest for the Loebner Prize, given to the designer of the machine that comes closest to passing the Turing test. So far, no computer programmer has won the grand prize.

The idea of a machine that imitates a human is a popular theme in science fiction books, games, and movies. One of my favorites is the 2013 movie *Her*[54], starring Juaquin Phoenix as a lonely young man who falls in love with the operating system on his computer, voiced by Scarlett Johansson. To Phoenix's character, the operating system is a person with a mind and inner subjective consciousness. The idea is not far-fetched. How many of us see Siri or Alexa as real people? We forget that we are speaking to a computer program.

There is a long tradition of humans trying to build a machine with a human mind. The Greeks developed the legend of Pygmalion, the sculptor who carved a woman and then fell in love with her. This is the basis of the George Bernard Shaw play *Pygmalion*[55], and based on this play, the Broadway classic *My Fair Lady*[56]. Of course, Mary Shelley raised the same theme in her classic 1818 novel *Frankenstein*[57].

My own Jewish tradition has dealt with the same question, can humans build a human-like machine? We gave a quote from the Talmud at the beginning of this chapter about the Rabbis building a human being. This story about Rava became the basis of one of the great legends of Judaism, that of the Golem created by Rabbi Judah

Lowe, often called by his initials, the Maharal of Prague (1520–1609). The Rabbi created a man called a Golem from the dust and used God's name to bring it to life, so it could protect the Jewish people. When Rabbi Lowe felt he was losing control of his Golem, he removed God's name and sent it back to dust. Tradition says he hid the Golem in the attic of the Prague synagogue. To this day people have visited the attic trying to find the Golem. Jews will often use the phrase "Golem" for somewhat dull-witted, who lacks basic sense. But the legend is about an artificial man.

Is the Golem truly human? Could we count him in the minyan? Would we be forbidden to harm him, let alone kill him? Is it even possible to make an artificial person? Is it a kind of Philosophical Zombie? We will return to this question at the end of the chapter on functionalism. But first we must turn to another materialist theory of mind: mind-brain identity theory. Perhaps the mind is simply the brain.

Chapter 6

Mary's Room: Mind-Brain Identity Theory

One of the oldest thought experiments is Buridan's Ass, named after the French philosopher Jean Buridan (1301-1359/62). Although he conceived the thought experiment, it had already been discussed by Aristotle and the Muslim philosopher al-Ghazali (1058–1111). A hungry ass (donkey) stands exactly halfway between two bales of hay. Because the ass is equal distance, the ass is unable to decide which one to eat. So, the ass stays in place and starves to death.

The paradox is meant to demonstrate the paradox of free will. Later the leading existentialist thinker Jean-Paul Sartre (1905–1980) would say that "Man is condemned to be free."[58] But if the mind is simply a machine, can such a machine have free will?

René Descartes taught that animals are mere automatons - bodies without souls. They are only machines with no inner subjective life. But to Descartes, humans are different. Descartes was a dualist who taught that humans have both bodies and souls, they are made of matter and mind. This fit into Descartes' religious view of the world. But materialism rejects this idea. According to Darwin's theory of evolution through natural selection, there is a direct line of descent from animals to humans. Darwin taught this in his second great book is *The Descent of Man*,[59] published in 1871. After reading Darwin we can ask the question, if animals are mere machines, are humans also mere machines?

This idea was laid out explicitly by the Enlightenment physician and philosopher Julien Offray de La Mettrie (1709–1751) in his 1747 book *L'Homme Machine*, (*Man a Machine*).[60] What is true for animals is also true for humans. Animals and humans are machines, which can be studied like any other machines. The mind is not something separate from the body, but something mechanistic, we can understand the mind by studying the brain. La Mettrie was laying the roots of what would become the second materialistic explanation of the mind, mind-brain identity theory (sometimes simply called identity theory). The mind is simply the brain.

Mind-Brain Identity Theory

In modern philosophy, one of the first to develop the identity of mind and brain was the British philosopher U.T. Place (1924-2000). In his 1956 essay, "Is consciousness a brain process?" Place challenges behaviorism's denial of inner subjective activity. Obviously. the mind and consciousness exist. We have an inner subjective self. He writes,

> ...statements about pains and twinges, about how things look, sound, and feel, about things dreamed of or pictured in the mind's eye are statements referring to events and processes that are in some sense private or internal to the individual of whom they are predicated.[61]

Mind activity exists. But to Place, it is identical to brain activity.

Place uses the example of lightning. Lightning is simply a stream of electrons that we can study. In the same way, consciousness is a stream of brain activity we can study. If we can learn enough about how the brain works, of which synapses fire under which conditions, we can explain all of consciousness. Place is not saying that the mind is identical to the brain. To be identical they have to be the same in every way. Clearly there are differences. But what he is saying is that all mental activity can be explained by brain activity. Learn enough about brain activity and we can understand everything about mental activity. Scientists seem to be getting closer to this ideal, using M.R.I.'s and other imaging techniques to map the brain, and often to map the mind.   As our knowledge of the brain improves, our knowledge of the mind improves.

Perhaps mind-brain identity theory was best expressed by the biologist Francis Crick (1916–2004), who co-discovered the double helix of DNA. Crick wrote in his 1994 book *The Astonishing Hypothesis*,

> You, your joys and sorrows, your memories and ambitions, your sense of identity and free will, are in fact no more than the behavior of a vast assembly of nerve cells and their associated molecules.[62]

Crick studies how the brain processes input, particularly visual input, to create a conscious image. Our brains are complex, probably the most complex things in the universe. There are billions of cells, each connected to thousands of other cells, But in the end, it is a fancy machine. The mind, consciousness, our spirit, are simply our brain. This became the prevalent view of many materialists. But it was challenged, even by other materialists.

One of the challenges to mind–brain identity theory is the question of free will. Let us consider the question raised by Buridan's ass. Can a machine make decisions? Does this vast collection of connected neurons have free will?

Determinism versus Free Will

If humans are mere machines, our minds mere brains, then we may ask a deep question. Can a machine have free will? Do we humans have agency, the ability to make choices? Does true volition exist? Or is free will merely an illusion, an example of what earlier we called an epiphenomenon? Recall that an epiphenomenon is a kind of illusion, where we sense that we have a will but that will has no real causal power. Perhaps we think we have free will, but in truth we have no real agency.

This is the idea taught by hard determinism, accepted by many (if not most) materialists. Hard determinism teaches that everything we do has already been decided by pre-existing conditions. Those who oppose free will bring arguments based on religion, science, and law.

The religious argument against free will has deep theological roots. According to classic theism, God knows everything. Therefore, God knows all our future behavior. God even knows what we will have for breakfast tomorrow. If God knows what we are planning to do, how can we say that we have free will? For example, God knew in the Exodus story that Pharaoh would harden his heart. Yet God punished him, bringing ten plagues. It seems unfair. The Rabbis of the Talmud appreciated this difficulty when they told, "All is foretold but freedom of choice is granted" (*Avot* 3:15).

One answer is that God does not know the future, only our inner tendencies. God knew that Pharaoh was stubborn and would probably not let the Israelites go, but the door is open for Pharaoh to make the right choice. Elsewhere the Bible teaches that humans can make choices. God says to Cain before he kills his brother Abel, "Sin crouches at the door but you can overcome it" (Genesis 4:7). Most religions are built on the idea of free will, allowing the possibility of sin or repentance. But if God knows everything, can we not say that God already knows whether we will repent.

Science also questions the possibility of free will. Neuroscientist Benjamin Libet (1916–2007), in a series of experiments carried out in the 1970's, challenged the idea that conscious decisions lead to physical actions.[63] He hooked electrodes to the brains of his volunteers, had them time the exact moment they decided to move their finger, then measured brain activity. He found that neural actions begin within the brain 350 milliseconds before the subject made the conscious decision to take such actions. The body has decided before the mind is even aware of that decision. Science seems to point towards the brain working on its own before the will kicks in. Volition is an illusion; the brain acts on its own. Of course, if the brain acts on its own, why should people be responsible for their actions? Why should we demand punishment for crimes if people have no control?

This is precisely the point made by the famous attorney Clarence Darrow (1857–1938) in one of his most noteworthy court cases, Leopold and Loeb. In May 1924, two wealthy young men, 19-year old Nathan Freudenthal Leopold Jr. and 18-year old Richard Albert Loeb, kidnapped and murdered 14-year-old Bobbie Franks in Chicago. They were trying to get away with the perfect crime. They had nothing against young Bobbie but were deeply influenced by the writing of Fredrich Nietzsche. He taught an ethics of personal power and avoiding what he called the "slave morality" of Europe. The two young men wanted to prove their intellectual superiority. But Leopold lost his eyeglasses when they dumped the body. The glasses were tracked to him, and the two young men were arrested.

Leopold and Loeb's families hired Darrow to defend the boys. Darrow was known for his rhetorical skills. Darrow recommended that the boys plead guilty to the murder and argued to prevent them from receiving the death penalty. He was able to convince the judge that the boys were not acting of their own free will. They were the victims of their own genetic predispositions and their upbringing. Let us quote part of his defense closing statement, where he famously argued that the boys were not acting of their own free will.

> Your Honor, I am almost ashamed to talk about it. I can hardly imagine that we are in the twentieth century. And yet there are men who seriously say that for what Nature has done, for what life has done, for what training has done, you should hang these boys....
> Why did they kill little Bobby Franks? Not for money, not for spite; not for hate. They killed him as they might kill a spider or a fly, for the experience. They killed him because they were made that way. Because somewhere in the infinite processes that go to the making up of the boy or the man something slipped, and those unfortunate lads sit here hated, despised, outcasts, with the community shouting for their blood.[64]

Darrow was able to save the boys from the death penalty. His argument is used by many who argue against punishment for crimes. After all, as the philosopher Immanuel Kant taught, "ought implies can."[65] We can speak of ethical behavior only if we assume people have free will.

One alternative to the hard determinism mentioned above is what philosophers call soft determinism or compatibilism.

According to this theory, both determinism and free will exist. One way to understand this is to say that our will is determined, but we are free to act on our will or not. Perhaps this approach was best summarized by the philosopher Arthur Schopenhauer (1788- 1860), "A man can surely do what he wills to do, but cannot determine what he wills."[66] I often explain this using the example of a drug addict. The addict cannot control the will to used drugs, but with great effort can control whether they act on that will. The entire recovery movement is based on such freedom of action.

Libertarianism and Existentialism

The opposite of determinism is the idea that we humans have free will. This approach is often called libertarianism. Setting aside all the scientific arguments that everything is determined, we have a deep sense that we have agency. As the poet Samuel Johnson (1709– 1784) wrote, "All theory is against freedom of the will; all experience for it." [67] We can make decisions and act on those decisions. Of course, this argument from free will seems to point to the notion that we are not merely machines. Our minds are not simply brains, acting according to chemical processes. Materialists will claim that this free will is an illusion. But it is a powerful illusion that is impossible to ignore.

In fact, there is a very popular philosophy based on free will called existentialism. According to existentialists, there are no excuses. We are free to create ourselves. As we already mentioned at the beginning of the chapter, Jean-Paul Sartre famously taught that "man is condemned to be free." It became a major movement in the second half of the twentieth century, particularly influential on college campuses.

Existentialism is based on the idea that we are thrust into a world, but we are given choices and can use free will to create ourselves. To quote Sartre once again, "existence precedes essence."[68] We exist and then we decide who we wish to be. According to many existentialists, we act in an absurd universe without any purpose. Many of the leading existentialists including Sartre and the thinker who influenced him, Friedrich Nietzsche (1844–1900), were atheists. But other existentialists, including the Christian thinker Soren Kierkegaard (1813–1855) and the Jewish thinker Martin Buber (1878–1965) were religious. All existentialists agree that humans are born with a radical free will and can create themselves.

If we have free will, can we say that the mind is just the brain? It appears to be something more. As we mentioned, various philosophers have also brought challenges to mind -brain identity theory.

Multiple Realizability

Perhaps the strongest challenge to mind-brain identity theory came from Hilary Putnam, the philosopher who gave us Super Spartans. Recall how Putnam challenged behaviorism by imagining super stoic individuals, who could feel great pain with no outward change in behavior. Inner awareness must exist. And to Putnam, such inner awareness cannot merely be brain activity.

Putnam developed a principle known as multiple realizability.[69] Any inner mental state can be realized in multiple ways among various kinds of brains. Let us suppose there is a particular brain state in humans when they experience pain. Pain causes certain synapses in the brain to fire in a particular way. According to identity theory, the mental state called pain is identical to this brain state. But not only humans feel pain. All kinds of animals also feel pain. But they have very different brains. So, the pain state for these animals would be different. Putnam uses the example of an octopus. We know from observation that an octopus reacts in a way that indicates pain. Yet an octopus brain is so different from a human brain that we cannot say the brain states are identical.

This argument can be taken further. Perhaps there is some sort of alien life made up of some totally different form of matter, perhaps green slime. Pain is a basic survival mechanism for living creatures, so we can imagine this alien creature feeling pain. But this green slime state would not reflect a brain state anywhere near a human brain. Or similarly, suppose we could create a robot made of silicon with a consciousness equivalent to ours. (We will discuss robots and consciousness in the next chapter.) Suppose the robot could feel some kind of pain when there was a threat to its body.

Silicon-based pain would certainly be different than our carbon-based pain.

The essence of Putnam's argument is that, if the mind equals the brain, then similar states of mind require similar brains. But it is clear that a subjective experience like mind can be realized by multiple kinds of brain. This is the heart of multiple realizability. The mind must be something different than the brain.

Philosophers since Putnam have discussed this issue at great length. But Putnam preferred an alternate approach to mind that allows multiple realizability – functionalism. We will turn to functionalism in the next chapter. But first let us look at my favorite argument challenging not only mind-brain identity theory but physicalism in general. We need to visit Mary's room.

Mary's Room

Australian philosopher Frank Jackson (b. 1943) suggested a famous thought experiment.[70] He imagined a brilliant scientist named Mary. Mary had lived her entire life in a black and white room and had never seen color. Perhaps we can understand her situation today, that she was totally color blind, unable to see any color. In spite of this limitation, Mary became the world expert on how the brain processes color. She knew exactly which wavelength of light could be seen as red, exactly which nerves in the eye reacted to that red light, and which neurons in the brain were activated when the color red was present. She knew exactly how the brain worked when it saw red, although she had never seen it. She could study a brain and determine, that brain is seeing red.

Then one day Mary steps out of her room and sees color for the first time. Perhaps using my understanding, she had surgery to cure her color blindness. (Note – color blindness is a genetic issue that cannot be cured by surgery. But this is a thought experiment, not meant to be taken literally.) For the first time in her life, Mary sees the color red. Until now she knew all the material details about how the brain sees red. But now she had learned something new, the subjective experience of seeing red. That subjective experience is different from anything Mary had ever known.

Philosophers call such subjective experiences qualia. We humans experience such qualia as seeing a rainbow, hearing a piece of music, smelling movie popcorn, tasting a cup of coffee, or feeling a kitten's fur. We also have inner subjective experiences of feeling joy, fear, or pain. Finally, we have the inner experience of free will, of making choices in our lives.

Mary's Room points to the fact that our mind is more than some physical object, identical to our brain. Subjective experiences seem to be of a totally different type. The mind is not identical to the brain. Materialists will need some other explanation for how the mind works.

The most popular such explanation, developed by Putnam and others, is functionalism. The mind is not a thing but rather a function, not a noun but a verb. The mind is not what the brain is but rather, what the brain does.

Chapter 7
The Chinese Room: Functionalism

One of the oldest thought experiments is the Ship of Theseus, with roots in ancient Greece. Imagine a ship traveling from port to port, and at each port having wooden beams replaced. Eventually all the materials that make up the ship would be replaced. At that point, is it still the same ship? The thought experiment asks the question of identity over time. Is identity based on the material components of a substance, or something else?

A modern version of the thought experiment was conceived by British philosopher Derek Parfit (1942–2017)[71]. He imagined a transformer that took apart all the particles making us up, sent instructions to a distant location, and reassembled us from new particles in the new location. This was precisely the image used in the television and movie series Star Trek[72]. ("Beam me up, Scotty.") When the transporter disassembles Captain Kirk on the Spaceship Enterprise and reassembles him on the surface of a planet, made of new "stuff," is he still the same person? Or as a functionalist such as Hilary Putnam would say, does the physical stuff of our brain really matter?

We are going to begin to explore functionalism by speaking of the mind as a verb rather than as a noun. We ought to begin with the thinking of the American physician, psychologist, and philosopher William James (1842–1910). James, the brother of novelist Henry James, is often called the father of American psychology. He invented the phrase "stream of consciousness" which sees consciousness as something that flows, almost like a river. The idea of stream of consciousness was extremely influential in early twentieth century literature, with novels written as a stream of consciousness (think *Ulysses*[73] by James Joyce.)

The Mind as a Function

Perhaps it is a bit unfair to include James in a section about materialism. He saw the world as more than material and wrote extensively about mysticism in his 1902 book *The Varieties of Religious Experience*.[74] He also argued for religious faith in his 1896 essay "The Will to Believe."[75] James was a pragmatist who argued that belief in God had pragmatic consequences, leading to a life of higher quality. For pragmatists, truth is not necessarily a reflection of reality, for we can never know reality. Truth is what works. (Later in this book, we will see the same idea expressed by one of the founders of quantum mechanics, Niels Bohr. Bohr supported quantum mechanics not because it reflects reality, a reality which is unknowable. He supported quantum mechanics because it works. Albert Einstein strongly disagreed. Bohr and Einstein would argue throughout their lifetimes. More about this later.)

Most important for our purpose, in William James' work on psychology, he wrote about the difference between the brain and the mind. The brain is a physical thing. The mind is not a physical thing, but rather a function. The brain is something that is, while the mind is something that it does. The brain is a noun while the mind is a verb. To quote his master work *Principles of Psychology* (published in 1890) he wrote, "A science of the relations of the mind and brain must show how the elementary ingredients of the former correspond to the elementary *functions* of the latter."[76] Note that he uses the word "functions."

For functionalists, the brain is an object, but the mind is a process. Perhaps this reminds us of the hardware-software relationship we mentioned in the chapter on Aristotle. In fact, some say that Aristotle was the founder of functionalism. He saw the mind not as a thing but as a process, the form of a body which animates it and gives it life. To functionalists, the mind is what the brain does. This is a total rejection of mind-brain identity theory, which saw the brain and the mind as two aspects of the same thing.

To the functionalist, each part of the body has its own function. The function of the heart is to pump blood, sending oxygen to all parts of the body. The function of the stomach is to digest food, removing nutrients that the body needs. And the function of the brain is to be a mind, thinking, observing, and choosing. Again, functionalism sees the mind as a verb, a process within the brain. Or to quote pioneer of Artificial Intelligence Marvin Minsky (1927–2016), "The mind is what the brains do."[77]

Human, Octopus, and Alien Brains

If James was the father of functionalism, philosopher Hilary Putnam was its strongest advocate of this approach. Remember that Putnam attacked identity theory based on multiple realizability. If the mind equals the brain, how could the same mind activity such as pain be instantiated in different kinds of brains – human brains, octopus' brains, green slime of aliens, or silicon chips of computers. For functionalists, it is irrelevant what the brain is made of. Mind can be instantiated in a variety of physical ways. But what is important for functionalism is not what the brain is made of but how it functions.

For those who have studied mathematics, one of the fundamental ideas is a function. In mathematics, a function takes input and produces an output. For example, the function $f(x)=2x$ takes a number x and doubles it. Using this function, 2 becomes 4. 3 becomes 6. There is an input and an output. Most mathematical functions are far more complicated than this. But they have the same structure, for every unique input there is a unique output. For functionalists, this is how the mind works. And in truth, this is how a digital computer works. We put in some kind of input and produce some kind of output. The computer could be made of silicon chips, nerve cells, or coconuts. The physical makeup of the computer is irrelevant. Putnam teaches that only the input-output, the way the mind ideally functions, is important.

Let me bring a quote from Putnam where he compares the mind to a machine. "If the machine is in state S_i, and receives input I_j, it will go into state S_k and produce output O_j (for a finite number of states, inputs, and outputs.)"[78] If this sounds like the Turing Machine which we described earlier, it is because they are the same. The mind is like a Turing Machine or a computer with input, processing, and output. It is a vision of the mind as a machine, the software of the brain. To functionalists, the mind is a kind of digital computer.

This description of the brain was attacked by a famous thought experiment conceived by American philosopher John Searle (b. 1932), the Chinese Room argument.[79]

The Chinese Room

Searle imagined a person in a room being passed cards with Chinese letters. The person would have a guidebook on how to respond to each Chinese letter. The person would receive the letters, look at the guidebook and then pass other Chinese letters out of the room. After some time, the person in the Chinese room would become so proficient that, to a Chinese speaker, it would appear that the person in the room was communicating in Chinese. But according to Searle, the person in the room does not know a word of Chinese. He or she is just following rules. (Searle's thought experiment is not an insult to Chinese speakers; it could be used with any language. I saw one professor use the example of Hebrew to demonstrate this to his students. It was fascinating to watch, because both the professor and I understood the Hebrew, but his students did not. Searle happened to pick Chinese.)

Searle, in his Chinese room example, differentiates between syntax and semantics. Syntax is the rules or grammar of a language. Semantics is the meaning. The person in the Chinese room understands the syntax, the rules to use in replying to the passed cards with Chinese characters. But the person in the Chinese room does not understand the semantics, what the words mean. He or she is following rules with no understanding.

Searle goes on to explain that this is the way a computer works. It manipulates symbols with no understanding of what those symbols mean. A computer runs a program, interpreting input to create an output, with no inner understanding. The problem with functionalism is that it sees the mind like a computer, something that manipulates symbols according to pre-established rules. But the mind is more than that. Unlike a computer, the mind understands what the symbols mean. According to Searle, functionalism must be wrong. The mind must be more than a machine manipulating symbols. The mind understands semantics, not just syntax.

The Chinese room thought experiment has been criticized. The main criticism is that the person in the Chinese room may not know Chinese, but the entire system – the person, the room, the input-output sources, as a complete system, seems to understand Chinese. We must look not at the person in the room but the entire system. Personally, I do not think the system understands Chinese. There is no mind there, just a person sitting in a room with a rule book.

We have looked at three materialist or physicalist explanations of mind. There is behaviorism, mind-brain identity theory, and functionalism. Each presents its own problems. Somehow it seems that there is more to the mind than something physical. But must we then return to Descartes dualism, which had its own problem? We need to look at a third approach, idealism. But first we must consider one more issue. Perhaps we build a machine that can truly experience qualia. Can we build a computer with a mind? A robot with a soul? To answer that question, let us consider the Lucas-Penrose interpretation of Gödel's Incompleteness Theorem.

A Robot with a Soul

Let us turn to a sophisticated argument that we cannot create a computer or a robot with consciousness. For those who love the popular science fiction trope of artificial intelligence, the android who is conscious, it is worthy of consideration. This is such a popular theme in movies and television shows like *I, Robot*, *Westworld*, and *Blade Runner*, it is worthy to consider whether we can build a robot with a soul.

In 1931, mathematician-logician Kurt Gödel (1906-1978) revolutionized mathematics. Mathematics works by algorithms, axioms and rules to prove theorems (think of high school geometry). To demonstrate what an algorithm is, let us look at a simple one – the thermostat in your home. The thermostat is set so that if the temperature falls below a certain number, the heater turns on. If the temperature rises above a certain number, the heater turns off. (Here in Florida, it is more likely to turn on and off the air conditioner.) It is a simple machine, with input and output. But every digital computer works using a more complicated version of the same thing. There is input, an inner process, and output. And according to functionalism, the mind is also the same thing. It is the software of a fancy computer, working by an algorithm.

Before Gödel, mathematicians assumed that given the correct axioms including those of arithmetic, we could prove every true mathematical statement. Given any mathematical system that was consistent (it cannot prove two theorems that are contradictory), the system can prove every true statement. Then Gödel threw a wrench into this simple, mechanical view of mathematics. He developed a statement which was both true and unprovable in the system. It was basically a statement that said, "This statement is unprovable in this mathematical system." It was a self-referential statement. I will not go into details here about how Gödel did it. Two excellent books which explain his method are *Gödel's Proof* (2001) by Ernest Nagel and James R. Newman[80], and *Gödel, Escher, Bach: An Eternal Golden Braid* (1979) by Douglas Hofstadter.[81]

Gödel proved that any consistent mathematical system which includes the rules of arithmetic contains statements which are true but unprovable. Any mathematical system is incomplete. But a digital computer (which we showed is a Turing Machine) is simply such a mathematical system. It works using algorithms. There are statements that are true but which the computer cannot prove.

Now let us turn to an essay by philosopher J. R. Lucas (1929 2020) entitled "Minds, Machines, and Gödel." [82] This was further developed by mathematician Roger Penrose (b. 1931) in his 1989 book *The Emperor's New Mind*.[83] This is known as the Lucas-Penrose argument. Could a computer or some other machine, using algorithms, have a mind? Or the flip side of the same argument, is our mind simply a machine, a fancy computer in our brain? Lucas-Penrose says no.

. If a mind is a machine, we can use Gödel's method to come up with a statement that is true, but unprovable using that machine. The mind would know it is true. But the machine could not know it is true. Since the mind is the machine, the mind could not know it is true. So the mind knows this statement is true and does not know it is true, a contradiction. To quote Lucas, "… for every machine there is a truth which it cannot produce as being true, but which a mind can. This shows that a machine cannot be a complete and adequate model of a mind."[84]

A mind must be more than a machine. Recall that Gödel used self-reference, the machine thinking about its own algorithm. Our minds can look inward and think about themselves. An algorithm cannot include itself in the algorithm, a computer cannot think about itself. Philosophers disagree about the Lucas-Penrose argument, but if Lucas and Penrose are correct, they seem to point to the fact that we cannot build a robot with a soul. At the minimum, it shows that our minds are more than fancy digital computers. So what is the mind? To begin to answer that question, let us turn to a third approach to reality – idealism.

Part 3: Idealism

We have explored dualism, the idea that both mind and matter exist as two separate substances. We have explored materialism, the idea that only matter exists. We found problems with both approaches. Let us turn to a third approach, idealism. Idealism teaches that mind is the ultimate reality.

Idealism has deep roots in Eastern religions. Hinduism teaches that the physical world is an illusion. There is one spiritual reality which Hindus call *Brahman,* everything else is mere appearances. Even our individual souls (*Atman*) have no separate existence outside of *Brahman. Atman* is *Brahman.* The material world is *Maya*, "illusion." Buddhism teaches a principle of detachment from everything in this world, which is transitory and bound to pass away. According to Buddhist doctrine, even our own souls have no permanent existence, but are *Anatta*, a term which can be translated "substance-less".

Idealism is less popular in the West, with its emphasis on science and empirical knowledge. Aristotle built his philosophy by studying the material world. But his teacher Plato, a dualist, claimed that this material world is a mere shadow of a more real World of the Forms. It is a spiritual world, accessible only to our minds. Plato comes close to dismissing this physical world as a place of impermanence and decay. His ideas would greatly influence

Western religion, who saw a world tainted with corruption and sin. For example, Gnosticism taught that this world was made by an inferior god and the goal of the soul is to escape from this world. Gnosticism became heresy in early Christianity but was popular in the ancient world.

Perhaps the most influential interpreter of Plato was the pagan thinker Plotinus (204/5-270 CE). He developed the ideas which became known as Neoplatonism.[85] The entire material world flowed out of a single spiritual source, which Plotinus called the One. Plotinus's image can be compared to a brook flowing from a spring, or the image I prefer, a punch bowl with the drink flowing from higher to lower levels. As this ultimate spiritual reality flowed into this material world, the One became many. But in the end, there is one spiritual reality behind everything. Much of Western mysticism, including the Jewish tradition known as kabbalah, grew out of Plotinus's ideas.

Nonetheless, idealism as an approach to reality was often ignored in the West. The one exception was the Irish philosophy and bishop George Berkeley (1685–1753). Berkeley, deeply religious, was fighting the growing materialism of his age. He famously taught *esse ist percipi* "to be is to be perceived."[86] Matter only exists when a mind perceives it. It a tree falls in the forest, does it make a sound? Not unless there is a mind to perceive it. Samuel Johnson famously kicked a rock with his toe, felt pain, and said "I disprove Berkeley thus."[87] But this does not disprove Berkeley; the pain itself exists only in his mind.

Bishop Berkeley's ideas seem radical to most philosophers in the West. But he also had his followers. Immanuel Kant (1724-1804), perhaps the greatest philosopher of the Enlightenment, is called a transcendental idealist. He divided reality into the phenomenal world of the mind and the noumenal world beyond the mind. But he taught that the latter was unknowable, we can only know the world within our own minds. Georg Wilheim Friedrich Hegel (1770–1831), the most influential philosopher of the nineteenth century, built on Kant's ideas. All human history is a history of mind, what he called *geist*, constantly transforming itself. This transformation of mind was known as the dialectic, a three-step process of thesis, antithesis, and synthesis.

Nonetheless, most Western thinkers believed there was a real material world of matter and energy. Then quantum theory came along and revolutionized Western thinking. Matter only exists when a mind perceives it. Until then, it is a superimposed set of immaterial probability waves. Is light a particle or a wave? Both and neither, until a conscious mind observes it. With quantum theory, suddenly idealism, the notion that mind is the ultimate reality, became important once again.

Let us study the idea that reality begins with mind. We will move several centuries before quantum physics, to one of the most brilliant minds in philosophical history, Gottfried Wilhelm Leibniz (1646-1716). We will begin by visiting Leibniz's thought experiments, known as Leibniz's Mill.

Chapter 8
Leibniz's Mill: Where is Mind?

Two monks were arguing about a flag blowing in the wind. One monk said, it is the flag that is waving. The second monk said, no it is the wind that is waving. Back and forth they went. Finally, they went to ask the great Zen teacher Hui Neng. He answered, my fellow monks, you are both wrong. It is not the flag that moves, and it is not the wind that moves. It is your mind that moves.

German philosopher Gottfried Wilheim Leibniz was a true polymath. A mathematician, he invented calculus at the same time as Isaac Newton. In fact, the two men argued about who conceived it first. A logician, he developed Leibniz's identity theory. If two items are identical, then every attribute of one must be identical to every attribute of the other. If the mind is identical to the brain, then they must be identical in every attribute. This is another argument against the mind–brain identity theory.

As an inventor, he created an early mechanical device which could add and multiply. As a physicist, he disagreed with Newton's notion that space and time were fixed and absolute. He felt that space and time only exist in relation to the elements within them. Today, based on Einstein's theory of relativity, we know that Leibniz's description of space and time is closer to reality than Newton's.

As a theologian, Leibniz dealt with the problem of theodicy or why evil exists. He argued that there are multiple possible worlds that God could have made. The fact that God made this one must mean that this is "the best of all possible worlds." Later in his novel *Candide*,[88] Voltaire (1694–1778) would ridicule Leibniz. He imagined Professor Pangloss ("all word"), speaking to his young student Candide who faced one disaster after another. Pangloss would reply, "all is for the best in this best of all possible worlds." *Candide* was made into a wonderful Broadway musical with a score by Leonard Bernstein. [89]

Nonetheless, Leibniz's view is often used to this day by those struggling with the problem of evil. *Our way is not God's way, and whatever God does must be for the best.*

Mind as the Building Block of the Universe

Most importantly for our purposes, Leibniz dealt with the problem of mind. Is the mind a machine, some kind of mechanical device? Leibniz imagined the mind as a machine from his day, like a water mill. This thought experiment is known as Leibniz's Mill.[90] If one walks into a water mill, one sees gears and various other moving parts. But there is nothing that corresponds to consciousness. Similarly, suppose we take this machine which we call a mind and greatly expand its size so we can walk inside. We would see moving parts, like a mill. But we would not see any kind of perception, cognition, or other kind of consciousness. We would not see a mind. Consciousness could not be something complex like a machine. Leibniz concluded, mind must be something much smaller or more fundamental.

This led to Leibniz's primary understanding regarding reality. Reality is made of small bits of consciousness, what Leibniz called monads. He developed his idea in his 1714 book *Monadology*.[91] Monads lack spatial extension but have perception and appetites. Although each monad is conscious, it is not aware of the consciousness of other monads. Each monad works independently. Nonetheless, somehow the monads act together in the world because God created a preestablished harmony. God, having created the best of all possible worlds, set it up so the monads act together according to God's will.

The importance of Leibniz's image is not whether it is literally true. Rather it is the claim that consciousness does not reside in some complex material object, like a water mill. Many scientists today claim that for consciousness to emerge, brains must reach a certain level of complexity. Leibniz claims that consciousness is much more fundamental, a basic building block of the universe. Consciousness is not an emergent property, but something more elementary to the universe. To Leibniz, the universe is made of small bits of consciousness.

Philosopher of mind David Chalmers claimed something similar when he taught that mind is a fundamental building block of the universe. As the universe is built of electrons and quarks, bits of matter, so the universe is built of monads or some other bits of consciousness. Mind is there from the very beginning.

Whitehead's Process Philosophy

Leibniz has introduced the idea that bits of mind rather than bits of matter are the ultimate building blocks of the universe. Future thinkers would build on this idea. One of the most important was British mathematician philosopher Alfred North Whitehead (1861–1947). In his 1929 book *Process and Reality*[92], he developed what he called a philosophy of organism, but what was later known as *process philosophy*. His work became very influential among many religious thinkers, both Christian and Jewish. Here it often goes by the name *process theology*. (An admission - I wrote my PhD dissertation on Whitehead and the creation story in Jewish mysticism.)

To Whitehead, the ultimate building blocks of reality are not objects like atoms, but rather moments of experience, what he sometimes calls actual occasions. He disagrees with materialism, claiming that ultimate reality cannot consist of soulless bits of matter which can only be moved by external forces. Whitehead was able to develop this metaphysical view by arguing that moments of experience, rather than particles of inert matter, are the fundamental reality. Each of these actual entities is influenced by all the other actual entities as it evolves. Here he differs from Leibniz, who taught that each monad is unaware of the existence of other monads. To Whitehead, all the moments of experience are aware of all the other moments of experience.

Each of Whitehead's actual entities is vanishingly small, existing for a very short duration of time, then vanishing. But, while each is alive, it is under the influence of all the other actual entities in the universe. According to Whitehead, each actual entity is also under the influence of "eternal objects," similar to Plato's Eternal Forms. And, when each actual entity vanishes, it becomes the basis of a new generation of actual entities. It is this interplay of actual entities, influencing one another, changing, vanishing while influencing the next generation of such entities, that Whitehead calls his *philosophy of organisms*. It is a world of constant motion and change, and this is the reason why Whitehead's system is called *process philosophy*.

Whitehead describes these fundamental building blocks of reality as follows:

> 'Actual entities' – also termed `actual occasions' – are the final real things of which the world is made up. There is no going behind actual entities to find anything more real. They differ among themselves: God is an actual entity, and so is the most trivial puff of existence in far-off empty space. But, though there are gradations of importance, and diversities of function, yet in the principles which actuality

> exemplifies all are on the same level. The final facts
> are, all alike, actual entities; and these actual entities
> are   drops   of   experience,   complex   and
> interdependent. [93]

These bits of experience, at a very low level of consciousness, become the ultimate building blocks of reality.

God takes on a different role in Whitehead's philosophy from the classical Biblical view. Whitehead defines God as an actual entity, but one that does not vanish. It acts as a lure for all the other entities, giving direction to the movement. Part of the value of process philosophy is it posits a God of persuasion rather than a God of coercion. God gives each actual entity a direction while leaving them free to act or not act on that direction. Personally, I find much power in this image of a universe built on bits of consciousness, given a direction in which to move but freedom to move as it pleases.

If Leibniz, Chalmers, and Whitehead are correct, that consciousness is fundamental to the universe, then how do mind and matter fit together? Perhaps each piece of matter, each quark and electron, has a underlying consciousness. Perhaps consciousness permeates everything. This is an idea under serious consideration by many philosophers (and some scientists) today. The name for this idea is panpsychism, pan meaning "everything" and "psychism" meaning mind. Perhaps everything has a mind.

If the panpsychists are correct and everything has a mind or inner consciousness, could this mark the return of Aristotle to

Western thought? The scientific revolution had banished Aristotle and his idea that everything moves according to a final cause. But science cannot explain the presence of mind in the universe. Perhaps everything that exists has some inner subjective desires. Alfred North Whitehead says explicitly that his process philosophy reintroduces Aristotle into modern philosophy.

What It's Like to be a Bat

Let us explore one contemporary philosopher who has written extensively on the idea of mind in the universe – Thomas Nagel (b. 1937). We will begin with Nagel's extremely influential 1974 essay "What is it Like to be a Bat?"[94] The essay is a criticism of a materialistic or physicalistic view of consciousness.

Nagel tries to imagine what consciousness must be like for a bat. He believes that most animals, particularly those higher on the chain of life, have some form of consciousness. But bats are mammals, closer to humans than lower animals. Yet bats use sonar to navigate the world around them. As humans, we cannot even imagine what it is like to be a bat. For Nagel, consciousness is "what is it like to be" something.

For Nagel, consciousness cannot be studied by science since science looks at the world objectively. He calls the scientific approach *the view from nowhere*, the name of one of his books.[95] But consciousness is not a view from nowhere. It is subjective, the view from somewhere, from a very particular organism. Nagel admits that as humans, we cannot truly understand the consciousness of another human. For example, a blind person can never understand what it means to see color. An alien who comes to earth to study humanity can never truly understand what humans comprehend in their minds. But the mind of a bat drives this home in a particularly effective way. How can we humans ever know what it is like to be a bat?

Nagel writes, "Reflection on what it is like to be a bat seems to lead us, therefore, to the conclusions that there are facts that that do not consist in the truth of propositions expressible in a human language."[96]   These are facts about the world that our science can never know. Science studies the objective world. But there are facts of the subjective world of consciousness, whether the consciousness of a human, the consciousness of an alien, or the consciousness of a bat, that are beyond the reach of science. There must be more to the world than the physical.

In his essay "Panpsychism"[97] from his 1979 book *Mortal Questions*, Nagel builds on these ideas. He claims that animals are made of material objects, atoms and molecules. Nonetheless, these animals have consciousness. Where does that consciousness come from? It cannot be explained by some material cause in the atoms and molecules. Nor can it be explained by dualism due to the problems we discussed in the chapter on Descartes. Therefore, according to Nagel, consciousness must be part of those fundamental building blocks that make up life. Atoms and molecules must contain some rudimentary mind if they are to be the building blocks of conscious organisms. To quote Nagel once again,

> If the mental properties of an organism are not implied by any physical properties but must derive from the properties of the organism's constituents, then those constituents must have nonphysical properties from which the appearance of mental properties follows when the combination is of the right kind.[98]

It is a radical idea, that all particles have some rudimentary level of consciousness. To be careful, panpsychism is not saying that rocks or your socks have an active mental life. But these items are made of elementary particles, which put together in the proper way, can lead to the emergence of mind. Mind seems to permeate everything. Or as Chalmers has taught, it is mind all the way down. But Chalmers is a dualist, that both matter and bits of mind are the building blocks of the universe. Panpsychism is a monist approach. There is only one kind of building block of the universe. Matter contains some rudimentary consciousness.

Nonetheless, there is a new question. If matter contains consciousness, then matter must be fundamental. But quantum theory raises new questions. Matter only exists when perceived by a mind. Quantum theory seems to point to the idea that it is mind, and mind only, which is fundamental.

Chapter 9
Schrödinger's Cat: The Mind in Quantum Physics

John Archibald Wheeler (1911–2008), one of the great minds of quantum theory, used a parable to explain the theory.

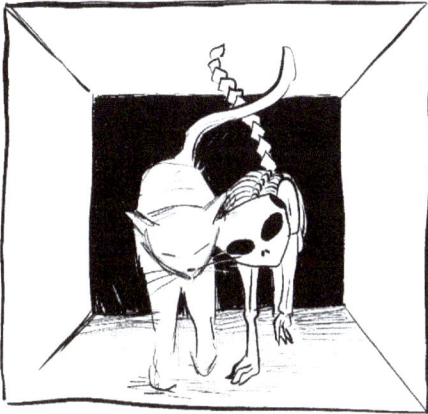

Three umpires are arguing. The first says, "ball, strike, I calls 'um as I sees 'um." The second says, "ball, strike. I calls 'um as they are." Finally, the third answers, "ball, strike. But they ain't nothing til I calls 'um."[99]

Any discussion of consciousness today must include the role of mind in studying the smallest particles of the universe. Quantum physics is strange. We can have electrons in two places at once, cats that are alive and dead at the same time, and particles instantaneously affecting each other across the universe. As Nobel Prize winning physicist Richard Feynman (1918–1988) famously said, "If you think you understand quantum mechanics, you don't understand quantum mechanics."[100] The mathematics is arcane and difficult. Nonetheless, it is perhaps the most accurate theory of the universe scientists have ever developed. So far, the experimental results have always been precise when scientists test the predictions of quantum physics.

Collapsing the Wave Equation

We cannot give quantum theory a full treatment here and we will stay away from mathematics. But we can share some basic ideas. Let us begin with the classical two slit experiment. Imagine a single photon (a particle of light) sent towards two slits close together. If we do not measure the photon, it will pass through both slits. Already this is strange, how a single particle can be in two places at once? The photon will create a wave interference pattern on the far side of the two slits. Imagine an ocean wave passing through two openings close together. It will create an interference pattern on the far side, with crests and troughs sometimes doubled and sometimes cancelling each other out. That is precisely what we will see on a screen, lines of light and dark.

Now imagine the same photon being sent towards two slits, but this time we set up a device to measure which slit it passes through. When we make the measurement, the pattern changes. It goes through one or the other, not both, like a bullet going through one slit or the other. There is no interference pattern on the screen. If we do not measure it, the photon is a wave. If we do measure it, the photon is a particle. The act of measuring and then consciously looking at the photon changes its nature.

This is often called the measurement problem in quantum theory. Mind changes reality. To quote the physicist Max Planck (1858-1947), who first discovered quantum theory, "I regard matter as derivative from consciousness. We cannot get behind consciousness. Everything that we talk about, everything that we regard as existing, postulates consciousness."[101]   It is as if consciousness creates matter.   We have moved beyond the panpsychist idea, that matter is conscious. Rather consciousness comes first, creating the matter.

Physicists use an equation developed by Erwin Schrödinger (1887–1961) to explain matter. Matter consists of a wave of possibilities superimposed on one another. For example, our photon consists of two wave possibilities, one going through each slit. They both exist at the same time. Only when a mind measures it does the wave collapse. Suddenly it is a particle, going through one slit or the other. Consciousness collapses the wave equation. It creates matter.

Until a mind collapses the Schrödinger wave equation, it is a sum of probabilities. We can never know exactly how the wave equation will collapse, only the probability of collapsing one way or another. This deeply bothered Albert Einstein, who claimed that "God does not play dice with the universe."[102]   He also famously asked a prominent quantum physicist, "Do you really believe the moon is not there when you are not looking at it?"   Einstein spent much of the latter part of his life trying to debunk quantum theory, as we will show shortly. In the end, Einstein was wrong and quantum theory proved correct.

The strangeness of quantum theory is perhaps best represented by a thought experiment developed by Erwin Schrödinger (1887–1961) known as Schrödinger's Cat.[103] Imagine a poor cat in a box, sealed with a vial of poison. There is a radioactive substance with a 50% chance of giving off a particle. If the substance gives off the particle, it will break the vial, poisoning the cat. If it does not give off the particle, the vial will not break, and the cat will be alive. Until someone looks in the box, the radioactive particle is a superimposed wave function with two possibilities, giving off the particle and not giving off the particle. Both are true. Therefore, until a mind looks in the box, the cat is both alive and dead at the same time. Only a conscious observer can collapse the wave function and decide the fate of the poor cat.

No one can explain this strange paradox. It is as if reality does not exist until a mind looks at it. This seems strangely close to George Berkeley's famous statement discussed earlier, "To exist is to be perceived." Berkeley used his ideas to prove the existence of God. God is the conscious mind that perceives everything and thus brings it into existence. Is there a mind of God in quantum theory? Of course, one could say that the cat has a mind. Perhaps the important point is that there cannot be matter without mind, that matter only exists in potential. An observer's mind creates matter.

There are more puzzles. In quantum theory, observation can never give us a full picture of the universe. Recall Laplace's Demon, who imagined an all-knowing creature who could predict the location and momentum of every particle. Such a demon would know the entire future. Quantum theory says this is impossible. Werner Heisenberg (1901–1976), another great mind of quantum theory, taught the Heisenberg uncertainty principle. We can never know both the location and the momentum of a particle. In the same way, we cannot know the exact energy of a particle with the time of a measurement. The more accurately we measure one, the fuzzier our measurement becomes of the other. Uncertainty is built into the universe.

We all imagine that there is a physical reality out there which we can come to measure and understand. Quantum theory teaches that our vision is at best rather hazy and unfocused. Everything is waves of probability until we measure them. But we can only measure with uncertainty. Our picture of the universe is like a motion picture out of focus, with no way to focus it. It is small wonder that Einstein disliked the theory. But our picture of matter is going to get stranger.

The E.P.R. Paradox

One of the pioneers of quantum theory was the Danish physicist Niels Bohr (1885–1962). Bohr was the founder of the Institute of Theoretical Physics at the University of Copenhagen, today called the Niels Bohr Institute. The entire theory of quantum physics we have been describing until now is known as the Copenhagen Interpretation, after Bohr and his Institute. (There are other interpretations of quantum theory, less well accepted by physicists.)

Part of Bohr's contribution to physics was to determine the structure of the atom. Usually, when a body orbits another body, it loses energy. In theory, when electrons orbit the nucleus of an atom, they should lose energy and eventually collapse. Based on classical physics, all matter should collapse. The universe should not exist. But quantum physics teaches that energy is quantized, it can only be released in set amounts. In higher orbits atoms can give off energy at these set amounts and move to lower energy orbits. But in the lowest orbit, the atom cannot release any more energy. It cannot collapse. The electron at the lowest energy level stays in place. All chemistry is built on Bohr's ideas.

Bohr had a long disagreement with Einstein about quantum theory. At a series of physics conferences in Solvay, Brussels, Einstein would bring a challenge to quantum theory and Bohr would respond. The history of this back-and-forth argument makes for fascinating reading. Einstein believed that there must be something incomplete about quantum theory; how could a particle not have a fixed location and momentum? There must be some hidden variables which exist, although we do not know them.

Then in 1935, Albert Einstein and two fellow physicists Boris Podolsky and Nathan Rosen developed the most famous challenge to Bohr's interpretation of quantum theory.[104] It is often called the E.P.R. paradox after the three scientists and its implications continue to this day. Let me summarize a form of the paradox suggested by a later physicist David Bohm. Suppose a source emits two particles, perhaps an electron-positron pair. Spin is a quantity attached to most particles, which can either be up or down. Spin must be conserved, so if one particle has a spin up, the other particle has a spin down.

As the particles separate, the spin is not fixed. Until a mind measures it, the spin is a superimposed combination of spin up and spin down. Let us suppose the two particles travel a huge distance apart, perhaps a light year (about 6 trillion miles.) Then someone measures one of the particles. It would take on a value, let us suppose spin up. Instantaneously, at a distance of a light year, the other particle would take on the value of spin down. The particles are entangled. Measuring one immediately affects the other.

According to Einstein's theory of relativity, nothing can travel faster than the speed of light. How did the information that the first particle is spin up instantly reach the second particle, telling it to go spin down. E.P.R. claims that there must be some hidden variables, some way each particle knows in advance whether it will be spin up or spin down. Einstein and his colleagues claimed that the act of measurement by a conscious mind was not the deciding factor, it had already been decided from the beginning which particle was spin up and which particle was spin down. Einstein attacked Bohr's interpretation, calling it "spooky action at a distance."

Bohr struggled to come up with an answer and defend his Copenhagen interpretation of quantum theory. But it would take the work of an Irish mathematician John Stewart Bell (1928–1990) that proved Bohr was right and Einstein was wrong.[105] There are no hidden variables; there is spooky action at a distance. It is as if two separate particles can touch each other instantaneously, even if separated by a great distance. Bell set up a mathematical inequality which must prove true if Einstein is right. The inequality has been tested countless times in laboratories and proven to be false. Particles can, and do, affect each other at a distance.

Entanglement is one of the greatest mysteries of quantum theory, forcing us to rethink our view of mind and matter. Physicists use the term non-locality, that particles have properties that are not local. Although it seems strange, particles can touch each other instantaneously at a great distance. Let us return for a moment to Descartes, the dualist who said that mind and matter are two separate substances. Matter is *res extensa,* a spatial thing. Mind is *res cogitans* a thinking thing. Mind is non-spatial. It has no particular location in space. One mind can touch another mind across a distance. And if the panpsychists are correct and matter has mental qualities, then matter can touch other matter at a distance. Bell's

Theorem, which challenged the E.P.R. paradox, seems to support panpsychism. Mind is non-local if matter has mental properties, then matter is also non-local.

The Implications of Non-Locality

What are the implications if mind is non-local; if minds touch one another over great distances? Up until now we have described main-stream scientific theories. Now we will begin to speculate on some stranger ideas. Some may call the material in this section pseudoscience. But there are legitimate scientists who take seriously some of the issues presented here. My own belief is that there is much that mainstream science cannot explain, most importantly, consciousness. Some contemporary thinkers have offered some revolutionary ideas, although the roots of those ideas go all the way back to Plato.

We will explore three thinkers in this section, the philosopher Ludwig Wittgenstein, the psychoanalyst Carl Jung, and the biologist Rupert Sheldrake. The first two worked at the beginning of the twentieth century, while the latter is still active today. In very different ways, they all taught how our minds connect to a reality beyond ourselves. There seems to be a universal mind with which our minds can connect.

Many consider Ludwig Wittgenstein (1889–1951) to be the most brilliant philosopher of the twentieth century. In his lifetime he came up with two totally different philosophical systems which opposed each other. His later philosophy will be of particular interest to us. But to understand it, we must look briefly at his early philosophy.

Wittgenstein was part of a group known as the Vienna Circle, who met and discussed philosophy before World War II. Their ideas centered on logical positivism, a materialistic approach to the world that taught we can only have knowledge of logic and science. All knowledge must be verifiable, either by the rules of logic or scientific experimentation. To speak of anything besides logic and science in nonsense. To the Vienna Circle, there was no room for any discussion of metaphysics, religion, aesthetics, or even ethics. As mentioned earlier, Wittgenstein said, "Whereof one cannot speak, thereof one must be silent."

Wittgenstein wrote out his early philosophy in his 1921 book *Tractatus Logico-Philosophicus*. He then decided that there was nothing more to be said about philosophy. He became a teacher of school children. Fortunately for the world, he was a better philosopher than a schoolteacher. He returned to philosophy and disavowed his earlier philosophy. Human beings need to speak in a shared language, about religion, morals, and art. Language is a shared enterprise which develops within a community. His ideas were eventually published posthumously in his 1953 book *Philosophical Investigations*[106].

Wittgenstein taught that there is no such thing as a private language. He did this through a classic thought experiment, the Beetle in the Box.[107] Imagine there is a group of people, each holding a box and each claiming the box contains a beetle. No one can see what is in anyone else's box. Wittgenstein claims that the beetle could mean something totally different for each person. Therefore, the word has no meaning. Words only take on meaning within the context of a shared community. Individuals could not invent a private language. Rather, language grows organically within the context of a shared consciousness.

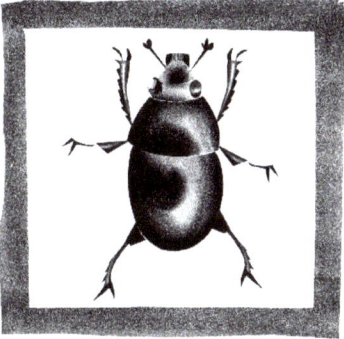

As Wittgenstein was developing his ideas about a shared language, Swiss psychoanalyst Carl Jung (1875–1961) was developing the idea of a shared consciousness. Jung was a disciple of Sigmund Freud, the founder of psychoanalysis. Freud developed the idea of a subconscious, a part of the human mind hidden from awareness but extremely influential. Jung broke with his mentor, partially over Freud's materialism and rejection of religion. For Freud, the unconscious was the id, inner drives such as Eros (the sexual drive) and Thanatos (the death drive) which people must learn to control. Jung disagreed with Freud by his belief in a collective unconscious. There is a reality beyond our individual minds. Our minds touch a spiritual world greater than ourselves.

Jung developed the idea of a collective consciousness.[108] That collective consciousness presents us with archetypes which are shared across multiple cultures. Cultures throughout the world share such images as the Great Mother, the Warrior, the Jester, the Sage, the Maiden, and the Lover. These archetypes are manifested throughout the world in mythology, religion, and art. Various cultures also share symbols. Water is a symbol of birth and fire is a symbol of destruction. It is as if humanity throughout the world shares a spiritual consciousness that exists beyond our individual selves. In many ways, Jung's ideas recall Plato's theory of the Forms.

According to Jung, as we mature, each of us goes through a process of individuation where we move beyond that collective unconscious to become our individual selves. Jung wrote in his 1964 book *Man and His Symbols*, "Man becomes whole, integrated, calm, fertile, and happy when (and only when) the process of individuation is complete, when the conscious and the unconscious have learned to live at peace and to complement one another."[109]

A contemporary thinker built on Jung's idea of a shared consciousness in a more radical way. Rupert Sheldrake (b. 1942), a British biologist and parapsychologist, has written a series of books which present some revolutionary ideas. Sheldrake teaches that there is more than a collective unconscious. There is a shared memory which influences not simply humans but animals, other forms of life, and the universe as a whole. He writes,

> The approach I am putting forward is very similar to Jung's idea of collective consciousness. The main difference is that Jung's idea was applied primarily to human experience and human collective memory. What I am suggesting is that a very similar principle operates throughout the entire universe, not just in human beings.[110]

Sheldrake gives this collective memory the name morphic resonance. Once again, the term morph refers to a shape or form, and the entire theory is reminiscent of Plato's World of the Forms.

He gives numerous examples of how members of the animal kingdom seem to learn from memories that are out in the universe. For example, he speaks of a kind of bird in England that learned to poke through the cardboard tops of milk containers left in front of houses and drink the cream on top. The idea soon spread to birds throughout Europe, as if they were tuned into a group chat on the internet. During World War II, milk was delivered without the cardboard tops. Nonetheless, after the war, although there was a new generation of birds, when the cardboard tops returned, the birds immediately knew what to do. It is as if there was a collective memory in the universe.

Sheldrake has written at length about how minds touch other minds although physically separated. One can see this in the title of some of his books. Two such books are *Dogs that Know When Their*

Owners are Coming Home[111] and *The Sense of Being Stared A.t*[112] Sheldrake has spent his career attacking the materialistic, mechanistic view of the universe favored by many scientists. He favors a more organic view; the universe is more an organism than a machine. Each part of an organism can be affected by an event happening elsewhere in the organism, even if separated by a distance.

Sheldrake accepts the idea of panpsychism as a step on the path to truth. Panpsychists claim that elementary particles, quarks and electrons, have a low-level consciousness. Sheldrake asks why larger, self-organizing substances cannot be conscious. He states, perhaps the sun is conscious. Perhaps the entire solar system. His work is a return to ancient animism, which anthropologist Edward Burnett Tylor (1832–1917) claims is the root of all religion. Everything, not just living things, are animated.

I have used the idea of the mind being non-local in my work as a rabbi. Regularly I am asked to pray for people who are sick, even if they live across the country. Why should my prayers in Florida help someone in a hospital in New York or Los Angeles? My answer is that prayer connects us to a spiritual dimension beyond the physical. Minds can touch each other across space and time. And perhaps my prayer can heal someone at a distance.

Why is the mind or consciousness non-local? Perhaps the answer lies in the Jewish mystical tradition, known as kabbalah. We will explore that in our last chapter.

Chapter 10
Holy Sparks: The Mind in Mysticism

Perhaps the strongest advocate of thought experiments was Albert Einstein. Many believe he invented his theory of special relativity by imagining he was moving beside a ray of light. What would he see? He also used a thought experiment to develop his theory of gravity or general relativity.

Walking to work, he saw a workman on top of a high scaffolding. He imagined the workman falling and dropping his hammer. Since Galileo had proven that all objects fall at the same rate, it would seem as if the hammer was standing still beside the workman as he fell. Einstein imagines what if an elevator and people inside were falling. Since everything falls together, would they even know they are falling?

What if someone shined a ray of light in the falling elevator. It would also have to fall. Gravity must affect light. That was a radical new idea. In 1919 during a solar eclipse, scientists proved that the gravity of the sun indeed bends light. Space and time, or what Einstein called space-time, is bent by gravity. Perhaps rather than our minds being in space-time, space-time is really in our minds. Perhaps mind existed before space and time.

Jews who attend synagogue regularly probably know by heart two of the most important prayers in their liturgy. The first prayer is the *Sh'ma*, which Jews say every morning and every night. Traditionally it is the first prayer a child learns while young and the last words one says before death. *Sh'ma Yisrael Adonai Eloheinu Adonai Echad*. "Hear O Israel, the Lord our God, the Lord is One" (Deuteronomy 6:4). The second prayer is *Alenu*, taken from the Rosh Hashana liturgy to end every service. It ends with the verse *B'Yom HaHu Yeyeh Adonai Echad u'Shmo Echad*, "On that day the Lord will be One and His Name One" (Zechariah 14:9).

Jews enthusiastically sing both these verses. They probably do not realize that the two verses contradict each other. Is God One now as the *Sh'ma* claims? Or will God become One someday in the future as *Alenu* claims? Should we believe Deuteronomy or Zechariah? How can they both be true? Quantum physics speaks of complementarity, two contradictory things both being true at the same time. Light is both a wave and a particle. Perhaps this is a religious example of complementarity. God is both One in the present and will become One in the future. How can that be? This idea became the basis of Jewish mysticism, the complex tradition known as kabbalah.

Kabbalah

Kabbalah breaks with the creation story in Genesis. At the beginning of Genesis, God through an act of pure will created a world outside God's self. The key idea is that God is separated from this world. The world is divided, made up of separate atoms and molecules. But God remains One. We live in a world of separations. This was the insight of Descartes who said that matter is extended, which means divisible. We live in a world filled with divisions. In fact, the creation story in Genesis is built on divisions. God separated day and night, the lower waters from the upper waters, the plants from the animals. But according to Descartes, mind remains indivisible. If God is One, perhaps God is primordial mind.

This idea of a world filled with divisions remained troubling to the ancient Greek philosophers. They taught a kind of monism, a unity behind everything. Heraclitus who we quoted earlier wherein we cannot step into the same river twice, also taught "Behind everything, one."[113] We saw in our study of quantum physics that non-locality is central to the universe. Things that appear separated across space touch one another. As one of the leading physicist David Bohm (1917–1992) famously said in his book *Wholeness and the Implicate Order*, "The notion that all these fragments are separately existent is evidently an illusion, and this illusion cannot do other than lead to endless conflict and confusion." [114] There must be an undivided reality underlying everything.

How can we reconcile the separation we see in the universe with the underlying oneness expressed in the *Sh'ma*. This was the goal of the great Safed kabbalist Rabbi Isaac Luria (*HaAri*, 1534 – 1572) when he retold the creation story. Luria's kabbalah is a radical retelling of creation.[115] It is a story where God, rather than creating a universe outside God's self, flows into the universe. In fact, perhaps the central idea of kabbalah is creation by emanation. According to Luria, how did God create the universe?

Isaac Luria's Creation Story

In the beginning there was simply *Ein Sof*, "Without End" or Infinity, an entity beyond all knowledge. Mystics often speak of *Ein Sof* as *Efes*, literally "Nothing." We can know nothing about this entity. This would allow mystics to speak in the same terms as philosophers, the universe was created from nothing (*creatio ex nihilo*). But the nothing for the mystics was not an empty vacuum. It was teeming with potentiality. It is fascinating how close this is to the idea in quantum physics that a vacuum cannot exist, it is filled with virtual particles coming into and out of existence.

Ein Sof filled everything. There was no room for *Ein Sof* to create a universe outside Itself, as Genesis describes. Rather, *Ein Sof* had to begin with an act of self-contraction, *Tzimtzum*, to leave room for a universe. *Tzimtzum* is central to the mystical ideas, only by self-contraction could God leave room for a universe to flourish. After this act of *Tzimtzum*, a divine light flowed into this empty space, filling the universe. The light was held in vessels that permeated everything.

Then comes a powerful idea known as *Shevirat Hakelim*, "the shattering of the vessels." The vessels could not hold the divine light and were broken – shattered, sending sparks of light everywhere. This seems very close to the central idea in modern physics that the universe was created by a series of broken symmetries. With the shattering of the vessels, brokenness entered the universe. To Luria, who lived shortly after the Spanish exile and inquisition, this brokenness explains the existence of evil in the universe.

With the shattering of the vessels, the divine light or divine sparks (*Netzitzot*) permeated everything. But they were covered by *Kelipot* "coverings." With the divine sparks scattered and broken, God's oneness became broken. God had been One but is now no longer One. God became broken. But all is not hopeless. We humans are able to uncover these Holy Sparks and help them return to God. In a sense, we humans can put God together again. The word for repairing the universe is *Tikkun* "to repair." *Tikkun* has become one of the most used, some would say overused, terms in Jewish life. In fact, for a long time there was a Jewish magazine on social justice and spirituality called *Tikkun*. The source of the idea is also a line from the *Alenu* prayer mentioned above, *l'taken olam k'malchut Shadai* "to repair the world as a kingdom of God."

The Lurianic creation story of *Tzimtzum* (self-contraction), *Shevirat Hakelim* (shattering of the vessels), *Nitzitzot* (Holy Sparks), and *Tikkun* (repair), have created powerful images in contemporary Jewish life. But what does this have to do with the topic of this book – mind? This was precisely the topic of my PhD dissertation. Let me make a radical reinterpretation of this story. Suppose the divine sparks were not bits of light but bits of mind. *Ein Sof* was the primordial consciousness, and the Holy Sparks were bits of that consciousness. According to this understanding, consciousness permeated the universe from the beginning. In speaking about creation, mind came first.

In my dissertation, I brought numerous sources that compare light and mind. How are we to designate or understand primordial mind? Already in Plato, mind was evoked by the metaphor of "light." Arthur Zajonc, in his book *Catching the Light: The Entwined History of Light and Mind*, writes: "Plato used sight as a metaphor for all knowing, calling the psyche's own organ of perception the `eye of the soul' or `the mind's eye.'"[116] In a similar way, Lawrence Wu writes: "Philosophers have long been using the metaphors `light' and `mirror' to represent the nature of mind and its functionings because of their richness of meanings."[117] Let us substitute the light at the beginning of creation with the mind at the beginning of creation. It was primordial mind that contracted and flowed into everything.

Sparks of Mind

The image of a primordial consciousness which is the source of all reality is part of many spiritual traditions long before Isaac Luria lived. (I want to thank Professor Seyyed Hossein Nasr of George Washington University for these insights. They were part of a lecture he delivered at Harvard Divinity School entitled "In the Beginning was Consciousness.") [118] The *Rig-Vede*, one of the oldest Hindu texts teaches, ""One alone is the Dawn beaming over all this. It is the One that severally becomes all this." (*Rig-Veda*, VIII, 58:2) The *Tao Te Ching* the sacred scripture of Taoism, teaches, "The nameless is the beginning of Heaven and Earth. The named is the mother of ten thousand things." (*Tao Te Ching*, chapter 1). And of course, the New Testament Gospel of John begins with the famous line, "In the beginning was the Word (*Logos*) and the Word was with God, and the Word was God" (John 1:1). *Logos* which means word can also mean mind.

A primordial consciousness which he called the One. was the central issue of the pagan philosopher Plotinus (204/5–270). He built on Plato's philosophy to develop a system of thought known as Neoplatonism. For Plotinus, the One becomes the many flowing into the world, as a spring becomes a brook which becomes a stream, which becomes a river. As it flows down, it divides up becoming separate on the way down. Part of Plotinus's concern is how our individual souls can climb up and reunite with the One. Many say Neoplatonism is the root of kabbalah and other Western mystical traditions.

Nonetheless, there is a difference between Plotinus's view of emanation and later kabbalah as developed by the author of the *Zohar* (attributed by scholars to Moshe de Leon) and Rabbi Isaac Luria. In Neoplatonism there is no volition or agency. A spring simply brings forth water without any decision to do so. There is no free will. To the Jewish mystics, *Ein Sof* has agency and acts through an act of will. In fact, the highest of the ten *Sefirot*, the traditional emanations from the One is called *Keter*. The Hebrew word means "crown" but it has come to mean "will." The universe did not happen by random chance but was created through an act of divine will or volition. As we wrote in an earlier chapter, free will is a vital part of mind.

Perhaps this idea was best expressed by the contemporary Jewish philosopher and expert on Gnosticism Hans Jonas (1903–1993):

> In the beginning, for unknowable reasons, the ground of being, or the Divine, chose to give itself over to the chance and risk and endless variety of becoming. And wholly so: entering into the adventure of space and time, the deity held back nothing of itself: no uncommitted or unimpaired part remained to direct, correct, and ultimately guarantee the devious working-out of its destiny in creation. On this unconditional immanence the modern temper insists.[119]

The key word Jonas uses is *chose*. God chose to create a universe, or perhaps better, to flow into the universe. It is an act of divine will. According to the mystics, creation is the emanation of God's very being into space and time. God is both beyond and within the universe. The fancy term for a God both beyond and within creation is panentheism. But if God is divine mind, then mind is both beyond and within the universe. Mind permeates everything. There is a divine spark, a spark of God, a spark of mind in everything. This fits into the panpsychism view of reality which we described earlier. It is not bits of matter but bits of mind which are the ultimate building blocks of the universe.

The Re-enchantment of the World

One can say that the goal of the kabbalistic retelling of the creation story is what some thinkers have called the re-enchantment of the world. According to German sociologist Max Weber (1864–1920), the modern world has become disenchanted by modern science and rationality. To quote Weber's 1917 essay "Science as a Vocation,"

> [Modernity is] the knowledge or the belief that, *if one only wanted to*, one *could* find out any time that there are in principle no *mysterious, incalculable powers at work*, but rather that one could in principle master everything through calculation. But that means the disenchantment of the world.[120]

Weber claims that the modern world views space as filled with mindless matter acting according to physical laws. We must reenchant the world by bringing back mind.

A world of mindless matter was not always the case. Many anthropologists believe that the original source of religious belief was a sense that the world was animated. As mentioned earlier, Edward Burnett Tylor, perhaps the first anthropologist of religion, taught that all religion grew out of animism. Animism is the belief that nature is filled with spirit and agency. Trees, rivers, winds, and the earth itself is animated with an inner consciousness. This seems to fit what is sometimes called the animistic cognitive bias to see agency in natural events. For example, we still give hurricanes names (we used to give them only female names) and act as if they make decisions. I heard on the news in 1992, "Hurricane Andrew *made the decision* to turn south and spare Miami Beach its most violent winds.")

If early religion was built on animism, that soon evolved into polytheism or the belief in many gods. And then with the Bible, monotheism developed. There was only one God. As the prophet Isaiah put it, "I am the Lord there is none else, besides Me there is no God" (Isaiah 45:5). Monotheism still teaches that this God intervenes in the universe, answering prayer and acting in history. The Enlightenment would see the transition from theism to deism, a God Who created the laws of nature but does not intervene in the world. God no longer plays a role in the day-to-day events of history. And as many have noticed, the jump from deism to atheism, the claim that there is no God, is easy to make. The history of religion becomes a line from animism to polytheism to monotheism to deism to modern atheism. God slowly disappears from the world like the smile on the Cheshire cat, and the disenchantment from nature begins. The universe is mindless bits of matter working by physical laws. No wonder Laplace could claim that if an all-knowing demon knew the location and motion of every piece of matter, the demon could predict the entire future.

Of course, there has been a reaction to this. The Romantic movement, responding to the rationalism of the Enlightenment, returned to a kind of worship of nature. Romanticism saw nature as a unified whole, not bits of isolated, lifeless matter. Nature could appeal to our emotions rather than simply be the object of manipulation. The Romantic Movement included philosophers, writers, poets, artists, and musicians. Thinkers such as Jean-Jacques Rousseau (1712-1778) and poets such as William Blake (1757–1827) sought to reanimate nature. Thus, Blake could write,

> "To see a World in a Grain of Sand,
> And a Heaven in a Wild Flower;
> Hold Infinity in the palm of your hand,
> And Eternity in an Hour."[121]

The Romantic Movement sought to reenchant nature. And today there is a return to what is called neopaganism, with such religions as Wiccan worshipping nature.

It is in the midst of this disenchantment of nature, kabbalah and particularly Lurianic kabbalah flourished. It sees a God not as separate from nature, but literally flowing into nature. Sparks of the divine are everywhere, waiting for humans to uncover them. It is a world not of dead matter but flowing with spirit. Such a re-enchantment of nature seems to fulfill a deep human need, part of the reason it is so popular today. To quote the Baal Shem Tov (1698 – 1760), the founder of Hasidism, "It is a great principle that there are Holy Sparks in all that there is in the world. Nothing is void of sparks, even trees and stones." [122]

Our Individual Minds

If mind permeates the universe, if the universe is enchanted as Lurianic kabbalah teaches, where do our individual minds fit in? The universe may be conscious, but what about our individual consciousness? Where do our minds come from? To answer this question, I believe there is much wisdom in Eastern spiritual traditions such as Hinduism.

Hinduism has a name for the ultimate reality we have been describing – *Brahman*. Everything comes from *Brahman* and everything returns to *Brahman*. Brahman is eternal, uncreated, infinite, and the source of everything. In fact, Hinduism teaches that the material world is *Maya*, illusion, changeable and temporary. Only *Brahman* is permanent.

Hinduism also has a word for our individual souls – *Atman*. The soul or *Atman* may temporarily die, but it is reincarnated into another life, its fate based on the *Karma* of a previous life. This ongoing cycle of birth, death, and reincarnation is called *Samsara*, a seemingly endless cycle. The eventual goal is to escape from this cycle of *Samsara* and reach *Moksha*, a return to the ultimate reality or *Brahman*.

Now we come to a central teaching of this Hindu tradition – *Atman is Brahman*.[123] Our individual souls are not separate at all.

They are part of the universal soul, the ultimate divine reality. We see ourselves as separate but beneath it all there is a Oneness. This is what Eastern religions and Western mystics have taught all along, that there is an underlying Oneness to everything. *Atman is Brahman.* This is also what physicist David Bohm taught when he wrote about the implicit order.

Perhaps the best metaphor for this idea is an ocean and its waves. Each of our individual souls is like a wave in the ocean. When a wave comes to the end of its journey it does not disappear, it simply remains part of the ocean from where it came. So our individual souls return to that divine reality.

This was beautifully explained by the Buddhist thinker and monk Thich Nhat Hanh (1926–2022),

> Let us look at a wave on the surface of the ocean. A wave is a wave. It has a beginning and an end. It might be high or low, more or less beautiful than other waves. But a wave is, at the same time, water. Water is the ground of its being. … The wave does not have to look for water, it already is water. Once the wave realizes that she is water, all her fear vanishes.[124]

The divine mind is a vast ocean and our individual souls are like the waves in that ocean. An individual wave may break on the shore and disappear. But it never truly disappears. It returns to the water from which it came. Our individual selves return to their divine source, like the breath of God returning to its origin.

Why are we not aware of living in this sea of consciousness? Perhaps another metaphor would help. Is a fish aware of water? If you ask an intelligent fish what water is, the fish would be stumped. When we live in the midst of something all-embracing, we are unaware of its presence. We humans live in a sea of consciousness and most of the time we are unaware. Only in those rare moments of mystical insight do we become at one with that Oneness of the universe in which we live.

Final Thoughts

We have now reached the end of our study of consciousness. We have looked at dualism, materialism, and idealism. We have explored a number of famous thought experiments.

Dualism, the philosophy of Plato and Descartes, is also at the heart of the Western spiritual tradition. It teaches that there are two separate substances – mind and body, that interact. But Princess Elisabeth of Bavaria already challenged this idea. How can a non-material thing like mind affect a physical thing like a body? Gilbert Ryle ridiculed dualism, calling it The Ghost in the Machine.

Materialism, the philosophy of most scientists working today, sees a universe of matter in motion. The universe is made up of atoms, mindless entities which join together to form everything that exists. But how can such mindless entities create consciousness? We looked at three answers given by materialists – behaviorism, mind-body identity, and functionalism. But Philosophical Zombies, Mary's Room, and the Chinese Room raised challenges to each of these approaches.

Idealism, the idea that mind is the ultimate reality, grew out of the Eastern religious traditions and also mysticism in the West. Quantum physics also points to the idea that matter only exists when mind perceives it. This suggests the idea that the basic building blocks of the universe are not bits of matter but bits of mind. Perhaps the Divine Sparks which fill the universe are really bits of mind that have scattered everywhere. Like an ocean, mind is the ultimate reality.

If this is true, we have reached an answer to our opening question. Mind permeates everything. Indeed, the universe does have a soul.

※

Endnotes

[1] Maimonides, *Guide for the Perplexed,* 2:25.

[2] https://www.imdb.com/title/tt0133093/?ref_=nv_sr_srsg_0_tt_7_nm_1_q_the%2520matrix.

[3] Descartes, Rene, *Discourse on Method.*

[4] Chalmers, David, *The Conscious Mind: In Search of a Fundamental Theory,* (New York: Oxford University Press, 1996).

[5] Bentham, Jeremy, An *Introduction to the Principles of Morals and Legislation.*

[6] Clarke, Arthur C. *2001: A Space Odyssey*, (New York: New American Library, 1968).

[7] https://www.imdb.com/title/tt0062622/?ref_=nv_sr_srsg_0_tt_8_nm_0_q_2001.

[8] Asimov, Isaac, *I, Robot*, (Gnome Pres, 1950).

[9] https://www.imdb.com/title/tt0212720/?ref_=nv_sr_srsg_0_tt_2_nm_6_q_A.I.

[10] https://www.imdb.com/title/tt0475784/?ref_=nv_sr_srsg_1_tt_8_nm_0_q_west%2520world.

[11] Dick, Philip K, *Do Androids Dream of Electric Sheep?*, (New York: Doubleday, 1968).

[12] https://www.imdb.com/title/tt0083658/mediaviewer/rm3676975360/?ref_=tt_ov_i.

[13] Chalmers, op.cit.

[14] Wigner, Eugene https://todayinsci.com/W/Wigner_Eugene/WignerEugene-Quotations.htm.

[15] Mermin, N. David, "Is the Moon There When Nobody Looks? Reality and the Quantum Theory," Physics Today, April 1985.

[16] https://www.reddit.com/r/Christianity/comments/phpmvp/you_dont_have_a_soul_you_are_a_soul_you_have_a/

[17] Yeats, William Butler, *The Second Coming*, https://www.poetryfoundation.org/poems/43290/the-sec(ond-coming.

[18] Shakespeare, William, *Hamlet,* Act 3, Scene 1.

[19] https://personal.lse.ac.uk/robert49/ebooks/philsciadventures/lecture24.html.

[20] https://www.jstor.org/stable/42743883.

[21] https://plato.stanford.edu/entries/anselm/.

[22] Whitehead, Alfred North, David Ray Griffin, and Donald W. Sherburne. *Process and Reality: An Essay in Cosmology.* Correct ed. 1927-28 Vol. (New York: Free Press, 1978), p. 37.

[23] https://theinvisiblementor.com/you-cannot-step-into-the-same-river-twice/.

[24] https://www.parmenides.me/.

[25] https://plato.stanford.edu/entries/protagoras/.

[26] https://press.uchicago.edu/ucp/books/book/chicago/V/bo18008895.html.

[27] Plato, *The Republic*.

[28] Plato, *The Phaedo*.

[29] Philo, "On the Cherubim," quoted in 3 Jewish Philosophers, Lewy, Hans ed. (New Milford, CT: The Toby Press, 2006), p. 40.

[30] Plato, *Timaeus*.

[31] https://phys.libretexts.org/Bookshelves/Astronomy__Cosmology/Astronomy_fo r_Educators_(Barth)/06%3A_Exploring_Gravity/6.03%3A_Galileos_Falling_B odies.

[32] In Latin *"Nihil est in intellectu quin prius fuerit in sensu."* Although attributed to Aristotle by Scholastic thinkers, I was unable to find the origin of this quote.

[33] Aristotle, *De Anima*.

[34] Aristotle, *The Nichomachean Ethics*.

[35] https://www.degruyter.com/document/doi/10.1515/elen-2023-0004/html?lang=en#:~:text=In%20his%20own%20De%20anima,of%20human %20intellection%20in%20particular%3F.

[36] Maimonides, op.cit. 3 51.

[37] Ibid. 1 68.

[38] Ibid. 2 26.

[39] Pope, Alexander, https://quotepark.com/quotes/1156445-alexander-pope-nature-and-natures-laws-lay-hid-in-night-god-sa/.

[40] Nozick, Robert, Anarchy, *State, and Utopia,* (New York: Basic Books, 1974).

[41] https://philosophynow.org/issues/76/Zhuangzi_And_That_Bloody_Butterfly#:~: text=According%20to%20the%20Chinese%20philosophical,dreaming%20he%2 0was%20a%20man.

[42] https://sites.psu.edu/bernickerpassionblog/2016/01/28/brain-in-a-vat/.

[43] https://www.thehumanfront.com/pocketsized-floating-man/.

[44] https://plato.stanford.edu/entries/elisabeth-bohemia/.

[45] Plantiga, Alfred, *Where the Conflict Really Lies*; *Science, Religion, and Naturalism*, (Oxford: Oxford University Press, 2011), p. 78.

[46] https://kwanj.files.wordpress.com/2016/02/ryle-the-ghost-in-the-machine.pdf.

[47] https://www.scienceabc.com/pure-sciences/what-is-laplaces-demon-definition-explanation.html.

[48] http://hyperphysics.phy-astr.gsu.edu/Nave-html/Faithpathh/Laplace.html#:~:text=Napoleon%20asked%20Laplace%20whe re%20God,constantly%20misused%20to%20b.

[49] Wittgenstein, Ludwig, *Tractatus Logico-Philosophicus*.

[50] Green, John, *Turtles All the Way Down,* {Dutton Books, 2017).

[51] https://www.youtube.com/watch?app=desktop&v=lRI95Vdc5CU. Jeffrey Kaplan has many excellent videos on philosophy of mind.

52
https://www.imdb.com/title/tt2084970/?ref_=nv_sr_srsg_0_tt_8_nm_0_q_the%2520imitatio.

53 https://plato.stanford.edu/entries/turing-test/.

54 https://www.imdb.com/title/tt1798709/?ref_=fn_al_tt_1.

55 Shaw, George Bernard, *Pygmalion*, 1913.

56 Lerner, Alan Jay & Frederick Loewe, *My Fair Lady*, 1956.

57 Shelley, Mary, *Frankenstein*, 1818.

58 https://www.goodreads.com/quotes/148810-man-is-condemned-to-be-free-condemned-because-he-did.

59 Darwin, Charles, *The Descent of Man*, 1871.

60 Offray de La Mettrie, Julian, *Man a Machine*, 1747.

61 Place, U.T. "Is Consciousness a Brain Process?" *British Journal of Psychology* 47:44-50. 1956.

62 Crick, Francis, *The Astonishing Hypothesis, The Scientific Seach for the Soul,* (New York: Scribner, 1994).

63 https://blogs.scientificamerican.com/observations/how-a-flawed-experiment-proved-that-free-will-doesnt-exist/.

64 http://law2.umkc.edu/faculty/projects/ftrials/leoploeb/darrowclosing.html.

65 https://www.britannica.com/topic/ought-implies-can.

66
https://www.reddit.com/r/QuotesPorn/comments/16dc6qa/a_man_can_surely_do_what_he_wills_to_do_but/?rdt=36757.

67 https://www.allgreatquotes.com/quote-397071/.

68
https://plato.stanford.edu/entries/existentialism/#:~:text=Existence%20Precedes%20Essence%3A%20Existentialists%20forward,are%20as%20our%20life%20unfolds.

69 https://plato.stanford.edu/entries/multiple-realizability/#:~:text=In%20the%20philosophy%20of%20mind,A%20common%20example%20is%20pain.

70 https://plato.stanford.edu/entries/qualia-knowledge/.

71 Parfit, Derek, *Reasons and Persons*, (Oxford: Oxford University Press, 1984).

72
https://www.imdb.com/title/tt0060028/?ref_=nv_sr_srsg_0_tt_8_nm_0_q_star%2520trek.

73 Joyce, James, *Ulysses*, 1922.

74 James, William, *The Varieties of Religious Experience*; *A Study of Human Nature*, originally the Gifford Lectures, 1901-1902.

75 James, William, "The Will to Believe," 1896.

76 James,*Varieties*, op. cit.

77 https://quotefancy.com/quote/1328351/Marvin-Minsky-Minds-are-simply-what-brains-do.

78 https://plato.stanford.edu/entries/functionalism/#CharInpuOutpSyst.

[79] https://plato.stanford.edu/entries/chinese-room/.

[80] Nagel, Ernest & James R. Newman, *Gödel's Proof,* (New York: NYU Press, 2001).

[81] Hofstadter, Douglas, *Gödel, Escher, Bach: An Eternal Golden Braid,* (New York: Basic Books, 1979).

[82] Lucas, John Randolph, "Minds, Machines, and Gödel," *Philosophy*, April – July 1961, Vol. 36, No. 137.

[83] Penrose, Roger, *The Emperor's New Mind,* (Oxford: Oxford University Press, 1989).

[84] Lucas, op. cit., p. 115.

[85] Plotinus, *Enneads.*

[86] https://iep.utm.edu/george-berkeley-british-empiricist/#:~:text=4.-,Idealism%20and%20Immaterialism,%2C%20which%20are%20mind%2Ddependent.

[87] https://askaphilosopher.org/2015/10/13/when-dr-johnson-kicked-the-stone/#:~:text=Boswell%2C%20in%20The%20Life%20of,'.

[88] Voltaire, *Candide*, 1759.

[89] https://en.wikipedia.org/wiki/Candide_(operetta).

[90] https://iep.utm.edu/leibniz-mind/.

[91] Leibniz, Gottfried Wilhelm, *Monadology,* 1714.

[92] Whitehead, Alfred North, *Process and Reality*, David Ray Griffin & Donald W. Sherburne eds., (New York: Free Press, 1978),

[93] Ibid. p. 18.

[94] Nagel, Thomas, "What is it Like to be a Bat?". *Mortal Question* (Cambridge: Cambridge University Press, 1979).

[95] Nagel, Thomas, The View from Nowhere, (Oxford: Oxford University Press, 1986).

[96] Nagel, Bat, op. cit., p. 278.

[97] Nagel, Thomas, "Panpsychism", *Mortal Questions*, op.cit.

[98] Ibid. p. 300.

[99] https://www.centauri-dreams.org/2008/04/15/john-wheeler-and-the-umpires/.

[100] https://en.wikiquote.org/wiki/Talk:Richard_Feynman.

[101] https://bigthink.com/words-of-wisdom/max-planck-i-regard-consciousness-as-fundamental/#:~:text=I%20regard%20matter%20as%20derivative,as%20existing%2C%20postulates%2.

[102] https://aeon.co/ideas/what-einstein-meant-by-god-does-not-play-dice.

[103] https://www.newscientist.com/definition/schrodingers-cat/.

[104] https://www.aps.org/publications/apsnews/200511/history.cfm.

[105] https://plato.stanford.edu/entries/bell-theorem/.

[106] Wittgenstein, Ludwig, *Philosophical Investigations*, 1953.

[107] https://web.stanford.edu/~paulsko/Wittgenstein293.html.

[108] https://en.wikipedia.org/wiki/Collective_unconscious.

[109] Jung, Carl, *Man and His Symbols*, 1964.

[110] Sheldrake, Rubert, "Part II - Society, Spirit, and Ritual; Morphic Resonance and the Collective Unconscious," *Psychological Perspective*, 1987.

[111] Sheldrake, Rubert, *Dogs that Know When Their Owners are Coming Home,* (New York: Three Rivers Press, 1999.

[112] Sheldrake, Rubert, *The Sense of Being Stared At*, (New York: Park Street Press, 2013).

[113] https://iep.utm.edu/heraclit/.

[114] Bohm, David, *Wholeness and the Implicit Order*, (Routledge, 1980).

[115] https://www.myjewishlearning.com/article/tikkun-in-lurianic-kabbalah/.

[116] Zajonc, Arthur. *Catching the Light: The Entwined History of Light and Mind*, (New York: Oxford University Press, 1995), p. 22.

[117] Wu, Laurence. "Light and Mirror: Two Mystic Metaphors of Mind." *The Philosophy forum* 14 (1974), p. 145.

[118] https://www.youtube.com/watch?v=fIjW1z-ZAX8.

[119] Jonas, Hans, *Mortality and Morality; A Search for the Good after Auschwitz*, Vogel, Lawrence ed. (1996: Evanston, IL, Northwestern University Press), p. 134.

[120] Weber, Max, *"Science as a Vocation"*. Tran. Michael John. Eds. Peter Lassman and Irving Velody. (London: Oxford University Press, 1989), p. 13.

[121] Blake, William, "Auguries of Innocence", https://www.poetryfoundation.org/poems/43650/auguries-of-innocence.

[122] "Jewish Environmental Perspectives," https://www.jcpa.org/art/jep5.htm.

[123] https://www.world-religions-professor.com/atman-brahman.html.

[124] https://thichnhathanhgems.tumblr.com/post/667877918653972481/let-us-look-at-a-wave-on-the-surface-of-the.

ABOUT THE AUTHOR

Rabbi Michael Gold retired from the pulpit of Temple Beth Torah, Tamarac Jewish Center in Tamarac, Florida in 2022, after serving there 32 years. Previously, he served as rabbi of Beth El Congregation in Pittsburgh, Pennsylvania and Congregation Sons of Israel in Upper Nyack, New York. Currently he has a part time position as the rabbi of Temple Beth Shalom in Century Village, Boca Raton, FL.

A native of Los Angeles, Rabbi Gold received his B.A. in mathematics from the University of California in San Diego. The Jewish Theological Seminary ordained him in 1979. He received his PhD in the Public Intellectuals Program at Florida Atlantic University in 2016, with a dissertation on process philosophy and Jewish mysticism. He is an adjunct professor of philosophy and religion at Broward and Miami-Dade Colleges in Florida and Charter Oak College in Connecticut.

Rabbi Gold has lectured throughout the country, in Europe, and in Mexico on sexual ethics, infertility and adoption, love and family, science and spirituality, and finding a mission in life. His articles have appeared in numerous publications, including *Moment*, *Judaism*, the *Jewish Spectator*, and the *B'nai Brith International Jewish Monthly*. He has developed courses on various spiritual topics for udemy.com. His weekly spiritual message goes to hundreds of readers of all faiths throughout the world.

Rabbi Michael and Evelyn Gold are the proud parents and grandparents.

ALSO BY RABBI MICHAEL GOLD

The Rabbi's Sex Class (ShelteringTree.Earth) 2023.

Three Creation Stories; A Rabbi Encounters the Universe (Wipf & Stock) 2018.

The Kabbalah of Love; The Journey of a Soul (Booksurge) 2008.

The Ten Journeys of Life; Walking the Path of Abraham, A Guide to Being Human (Simcha Press) 2007.

*God, Love, Sex, and Family; A Rabbi's Guide for Building Relationships (*Jason Aronson Inc.) 1998.

Does God Belong in the Bedroom? (The Jewish Publication Society) 1992.

And *Hannah Wept; Infertility, Adoption, and the Jewish Couple* (The Jewish Publication Society) 1988.

ShelteringTreeMedia.com